Goodheart-Willcox's BUILD-A-COURSE Series

woodworking

by

WILLIS H. WAGNER

Professor, Industrial Arts, Technology
University of Northern Iowa, Cedar Falls

WALTER C. BROWN, Consulting Editor

Professor, Division of Technology
Arizona State University, Tempe

Books in Build-A-Course Series

Drafting — Brown

Woodworking — Wagner

Metalworking — Boyd

Electricity — Gerrish

Graphic Arts — Kagy

Power Mechanics — Atteberry

Leathercraft — Zimmerman

Plastics — Cope

Modern General Shop

South Holland, Illinois

THE GOODHEART-WILLCOX COMPANY, INC.

Publishers

INTRODUCTION

This Build-A-Course text in WOODWORKING is a first or exploratory course. It provides instruction and information concerning tools, machines and materials that are basic to the broad area of woodwork.

Hand tool operations are stressed since the beginning students will be using them for most of their work. Only the most basic power machine operations that are practical in a beginning course have been included. An important unit on wood finishing provides instruction on the application of modern finishing materials that are adaptable to the school shop.

The importance of careful planning and good design is emphasized. A number of shop tested projects are presented. They range from "starter" projects, where complete plans are provided, to elective projects where only a photograph and overall size suggestions are given.

A number of jigs and special setups are shown that will help the inexperienced students perform difficult operations with speed and accuracy. They will also give students some appreciation of procedures used in production woodwork.

The importance of safe work habits and practices in using both hand tools and power machines is stressed by listing of safety rules, as well as concise directions in operational procedures.

TO THE STUDENT

Wood is one of our greatest natural resources and is used to construct our homes, furniture and many articles that we use every day. More than a million people are employed in trades and industries directly related to wood and wood products.

Woodworking has always been of great interest to young people, for learning about wood and how to use tools and machines is a fascinating experience. Added to this is the personal satisfaction that comes from the actual construction of attractive and useful projects with equipment that is similar to that used in industry.

In this course you will learn to thoughtfully plan your work, as well as develop important skills in using tools and machines. Furthermore, you will develop an appreciation for good workmanship. You will experience pride in building things for yourself and others. Very likely, you will want to develop a shop area at home where you can continue to enjoy woodworking as a hobby. You may also want to consider the many important and interesting careers offered by the wood and wood products industry.

Willis Wagner

Library of Congress Cataloging in Publication Data
Wagner, Willis H.
   Woodworking.
   (Goodheart-Willcox's build-a-course series)
   Includes index.
   SUMMARY: An introductory text for a basic course in woodworking, stressing hand tool operations, the importance of planning and design, and safe work habits.
   1. Woodwork. [1. Woodwork]
I. Brown, Walter Charles, II. Title.
TT180.W28   1981   684'.08   80–27505
ISBN 0–87006–316–2

CONTENTS

Unit 1 — PLANNING YOUR WORK 4

Unit 2 — SELECTING AND ROUGHING OUT STOCK 10

Unit 3 — PLANING AND SAWING STOCK TO
FINISHED DIMENSIONS 15

Unit 4 — MAKING WOOD JOINTS 21

Unit 5 — FORMING CURVES, CHAMFERS, BEVELS 27

Unit 6 — DRILLING AND BORING HOLES 32

Unit 7 — CLAMPING AND GLUING WOOD 37

Unit 8 — METAL FASTENERS FOR WOODWORK 41

Unit 9 — SANDING AND PREPARING FOR FINISH 45

Unit 10 — WOOD FINISHING 50

Unit 11 — DRILL PRESS, JIG SAW, BAND SAW 58

Unit 12 — JOINTER, CIRCULAR SAW 64

Unit 13 — WOOD LATHE 71

Unit 14 — WOOD, LUMBER, FOREST PRODUCTS 77

Unit 15 — CAREER OPPORTUNITIES 85

Unit 16 — WOODWORKING PROJECTS 89

GLOSSARY 113

METRIC SYSTEM 116

INDEX 118

PLANNING YOUR WORK

UNIT 1

TODAY LET'S STUDY

1. Why it is important to plan your work.
2. What things you should consider when selecting a woodworking project.
3. How to make pictorial sketches of project ideas.
4. How to make a plan of procedure and bill of material.

Planning is thinking through an activity, or undertaking, before starting it. It may be as simple as developing a schedule for the day, or as complicated as planning a new school building or a new jet airliner. The engineering departments of industrial organizations deal with such planning activities as: product selection and design, equipment selection and plant layout, production sequence and timing, and estimating costs of a new product. They realize that careful planning will save time, energy, materials, and will insure a good product, Fig. 1-1.

Planning is a very important part of your work in the school shop. Mass production projects, Fig. 1-2, usually include all of the activities employed by industry. Careful planning will help you avoid mistakes and get more work done. And you will seldom need to ask your instructor "What do I do next?"

A complete planning operation in woodwork includes the following steps: selecting a project, making a pictorial sketch, developing or refining the design, making a working drawing, preparing a step-by-step procedure, listing tools and machines that will be used for the work and preparing a bill (list) of material. See Figs. 1-1 and 1-2.

SELECTING PROJECTS

If this is your first course in the shop, your instructor will probably assign your first project and provide you with the plans you need.

For your second or third project, you may have an opportunity to select from a group of projects. You probably will be expected to develop some of the planning materials. As you gain experience and develop ability in your shop work, you will want to select and plan your own projects (with the help of your instructor).

When you select a project you must consider the following: how much time it will take, your ability, are the tools and materials available, how much will it cost, is there space to store it during construction, is it something you need or will enjoy building. If it is an article for your home you should secure your parents' ideas on style, color, finish or size.

Beginning students may tend to overestimate their ability and may undertake projects that are too difficult. It is not satisfying to "wind-up" at the end of the term with half-finished projects.

There are many sources for woodworking projects and ideas. Your shop or school library should be

Fig. 1-1. Planning an equipment layout for a new industrial plant.   (Viking Pump Co.)

Fig. 1-2. Careful planning insures success of mass production projects. View shows main assembly station for a peg-game board. Assembly jigs are mounted on a panel that is revolved counterclockwise.

checked. Stores and gift shops show many articles made of wood. Homecraft and household magazines offer ideas for shop projects.

PROJECT DESIGN

The things you make in the shop should be well designed. They should serve the purpose for which they were intended and be attractive in appearance. The finest workmanship and finish will not "make-up" for poor design.

Learning to recognize good design will take time and effort. You should know some of the simple rules concerning balance, proportion and unity. One of the best ways to improve your ability along this line is to study objects that are well designed.

Today, designers place great emphasis on function (usefulness). They also look for: smooth, trim lines; simple shapes and forms; and interesting grain patterns, colors and textures. They are cautious about using extra shapes, carvings and inlays just to add to the appearance.

Check the design you have selected or developed to see if it is the correct size. A book rack should be the right size for the books it will hold. The height of

a coffee table or foot stool must be correct for its use. There are many "standard sizes" you should consider.

The size of the parts of the project and the way the parts are fitted together should be correct for your design. For example, the size of a table leg should be just large enough to give the strength needed. To make it larger will waste material and cause a "clumsy" appearance. Be sure the joints will provide enough strength to hold the parts together.

Ask yourself some of these questions about your project design: What will it be used for and will it serve this purpose? Is it constructed in the simplest and most practical way? Are the sizes and kinds of material the best for this design? Will it fit into the surroundings where it will be used? Will it be easy to use and care for? Will it look as good to me next year as it does now?

MAKING A PICTORIAL SKETCH

As you work with your project ideas, pictorial sketches will help you record your ideas. They do not take long to make, and are a good way to show your instructor what you have in mind as you secure his approval and suggestions.

5

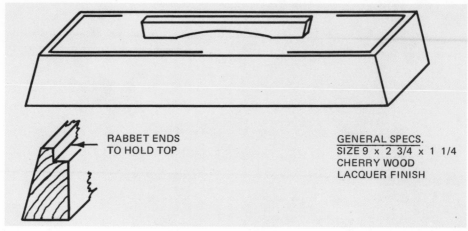

Fig. 1-3. Pictorial drawing of a card box.

RABBET ENDS
TO HOLD TOP

GENERAL SPECS.
SIZE 9 x 2 3/4 x 1 1/4
CHERRY WOOD
LACQUER FINISH

One of the simplest forms of pictorial drawing is called cabinet drawing. An example is shown in Fig. 1-3. First make a profile view or front view, and then secure the third dimension (picture effect) by drawing back at an angle. Show only the outline that you can see. Make the lines drawn at an angle only about half their actual length. Pictorial views are hard to dimension and it is usually easiest to list the over-all sizes in note form as shown in the example.

You will probably need to make several drawings before you have one that is satisfactory. As you make a second drawing, use the procedure of tracing the best part of your first drawing. If you make this "overlay" with a good grade of bond paper you will be able to see the lines of your first drawing. A standard 8 1/2 x 11 sheet of paper (draftsmen call it an A size) will be a good size for most of your work.

WORKING DRAWINGS

After you have secured approval of your project ideas, you are ready to develop a working drawing. This is a drawing such as shown in Fig. 1-4. See also Fig. 1-5. It gives complete size and shape description through the use of several views and dimension lines. Detail views (usually drawn larger) show just how the object will be put together.

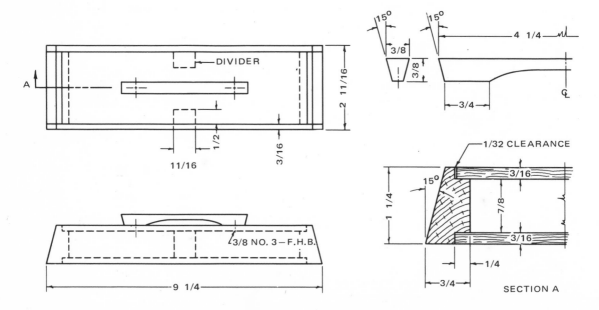

Fig. 1-4. Working drawing of a card box.

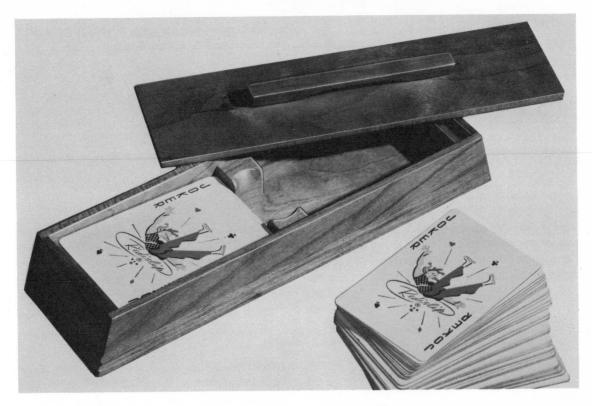

Fig. 1-5. Photograph of completed card box.

Making a good working drawing requires a lot of "know how" and skill and is a study in itself. If you need to prepare a working drawing before you have any experience in this area you should study a drawing textbook (there is one available in this series). From this study you should be able to make a rough shop sketch that will guide you through the construction of your project. Later, you may want to prepare a finished working drawing as a part of your elective work in the drawing area.

MAKING A PLAN OF PROCEDURE

A plan of procedure is a carefully prepared list of the steps you will follow in the construction of your project. It will require a careful study of your drawings to recognize the various operations and work ahead of you. This is one of the very important parts of your project plans for it will help you organize your work from day to day and prevent mistakes.

The steps should be listed in outline form. The list should not be too brief; neither should it be too long and detailed. Usually listing the exact operations and defining the part involved will be sufficient.

CARD BOX PLAN OF PROCEDURE

1. Make a stock-cutting list.
2. Select and cut out the stock.
3. Make the end pieces.
   a. Surface one side.
   b. Plane to finished width.
   c. Cut the rabbet joints while the stock is in one piece.
   d. Cut the pieces to finished length.
4. Make the sides, top and bottom.
   a. Surface rough cutting on one side if necessary.
   b. Rip to rough width and plane to finished width.
   c. Square pieces to finished length.
5. Sand the inside surfaces of all parts.
6. Glue the bottom and ends together.
7. Trim the bottom and ends if they do not line-up exactly.
8. Glue on the sides and fit the top in "dry."
9. Surface the outside of the box and cut the ends to the required angle.
10. Sand the outside surfaces. Remove the lid and sand the required clearance.
11. Make and glue in the dividers.

12. Make and attach the lid handle.
13. Remove the handle and prepare the surface for finish.
14. Apply a sealer to all surfaces.
15. Rub down sealer and apply two coats of lacquer to all outside surfaces.
16. Attach handle.

MAKING A BILL OF MATERIAL

A bill of material is a list of the things you need to build the project. The items will include: number of pieces, exact size (including joints), kind of wood and name of the part. List the dimensions of your stock in this order: thickness x width x length. The width is the dimension across the grain, the length is along the grain. A piece of stock could be wider than it is long. A complete bill of material includes hardware and finishing materials.

No.	Size	Kind	Part
2 pcs.	3/4 x 1 1/4 x 2 5/16	Cherry	Ends
2 pcs.	1/4 x 2 5/16 x 8 1/4	Cherry	Bottom & Top
2 pcs.	1/4 x 1 1/4 x 9 1/4	Cherry	Sides
1 pc.	3/8 x 3/8 x 4 1/4	Cherry	Handle
1 pc.	1/2 x 7/8 x 11/16	Cherry	Divider
2	3/8 – No. 3 – F.H.B.		Wood Screws
	Sealer and Lacquer		

Bill of material for card box (Fig. 1-5).

A stock-cutting list can be developed from the bill of material. It is useful for estimating costs and checking out your lumber. Add about 1/16 in. to the thickness dimension if the stock must be planed. The width should be increased from 1/8 to 1/4 in. and the length about 1/2 to 1 in. Try to group the parts together as much as possible. Stock-cutting lists may vary for a given bill of material depending on the sizes of lumber that are available. A sample stock-cutting list for the card box is listed below:

No.	Size	Kind	Parts
1 pc.	5/16 x 4 x 20	Cherry	Sides, Top & Bottom
1 pc.	13/16 x 1 1/2 x 8	Cherry	Ends and Divider
1 pc.	3/8 x 3/8 x 6	Cherry	Handle

Stock-cutting list for card box.

These sizes can be used to estimate the cost of the wood. The actual cost may be somewhat more, depending on sizes that are available in the stock room. For example, you may be required to purchase a 2 in. width for the second item in the list.

QUIZ – UNIT 1

(Write answers on separate sheet of paper. Do not write in this book.)

1. Planning operations in the school shop may include: selecting a project; developing the design; making a pictorial drawing; making a working drawing; making a _____ _____ _____; and developing tool and material lists.
2. A good way to improve your ability to design problems is to _____ objects that are well designed.
3. When we refer to an object as being functional, we mean that it is _____.
4. In a cabinet drawing the lines drawn at an angle are made _____ their actual length.
5. The draftsman refers to an 8 1/2 x 11 in. drawing as an _____ size.
6. A working drawing shows the exact shape and _____ of an object.

Total eye protection includes the use of safety glasses and shields along with enough good light to see what you are doing without straining your eyes.

GENERAL SAFETY RULES

SAMMY SAFETY Says:

"An important part of your experience in woodworking will be learning to follow safe practices and procedures that will prevent injuries to <u>yourself and others</u>. Give close attention to the instructions and demonstrations given by your instructor and study the directions for using tools listed in this book. As you learn to use a tool the correct way, you are also learning to use it the safest way.

Study and learn the safety rules listed below. Your instructor may recommend some additional ones that apply to a specific shop. It is desirable for you to be highly interested in your work but you must guard against becoming so "wrapped-up" in it that you forget to work safely.

SECURE APPROVAL: Secure the instructor's approval for all work you plan to do in the shop. He or she is the one to decide if the work can and should be done and will be able to suggest the best, easiest and safest way to do it.

CLOTHING: Dress properly for your work. Remove coats, sweaters, and jackets; tuck in your tie and roll up your sleeves. It is advisable to wear a shop apron.

EYE PROTECTION: Wear safety goggles or a face shield when doing any operation that may endanger your eyes. Be sure you have enough good light to see what you are doing without straining your eyes.

CLEAN HANDS: Keep your hands clean and free of oil or grease. You will do better and safer work, and the tools and your project work will stay in good condition.

CONSIDERATION OF OTHERS: Be thoughtful and helpful toward other students in the class. Caution them if they are violating a safety rule.

TOOL SELECTION: Select the proper size and type of tool for your work. Use only tools that are sharp and in good condition. Inform your instructor if tools are broken, have loose handles, or need adjustments.

CARRYING TOOLS: Keep edged and pointed tools turned down and do not swing your arms or raise them over your head while carrying them. Do not carry sharp tools in your pockets.

CLAMPING STOCK: Wherever possible, mount your work in a vise or clamp it to a bench. This is especially important when using chisels, gouges or carving tools.

USING TOOLS: Hold a tool in the correct position while using it. Most edged tools should be held in both hands with the cutting motion away from yourself and other students. Be careful when using your hand or fingers as a guide to start a cut. Test the sharpness of a tool with a strip of paper or a scrap of wood. Do not use your fingers.

BENCH ORGANIZATION: Keep your project material carefully organized on your bench with tools located near the center. Do not "pile" tools on top of each other. Never allow edged or pointed tools to extend out over the edge of the bench. Close your vise when it is not in use and see that the handle is turned down. Keep drawers and cabinet doors closed.

FLOOR SAFETY: The floor should be clear of scrap blocks and excessive litter. Keep projects, sawhorses and other equipment and materials you are using out of traffic lanes. Wipe up immediately any liquids spilled on the floor.

MATERIAL AND PROJECT STORAGE: Store and stack your project work carefully. Straighten the lumber rack when you remove a board. Do not leave narrow strips protruding from the end of the rack, especially at or near eye level.

LIFTING: Protect your back muscles when lifting heavy objects. Have someone help you and lift with your arm and leg muscles. Secure help with long boards, even though they are not heavy.

FIRE PROTECTION: Apply and handle finishing materials only in approved areas. Close cans of finishing materials and thinners immediately after use. Use flammable liquids in very small quantities. Be sure the container is labeled. Dispose of oily rags and other combustible materials immediately or store them in an approved container. Secure the instructor's approval before you bring any flammable liquids into the shop.

INJURIES: Report all injuries, even though slight, to your instructor."

SELECTING AND ROUGHING-OUT STOCK

UNIT 2

1. How wood is classified and graded.
2. How to figure the number of board feet in a piece of stock.
3. How to lay out rough sizes and cut them with the hand saw.

KINDS OF WOOD

Trees are classified either as softwood or hardwood. Softwoods are the evergreen or needle-bearing trees and are often called "conifers" because many of them bear cones. Hardwood comes from broad-leafed (deciduous) trees that shed their leaves each fall. This classification is a little confusing because some of the hardwood trees produce a softer textured wood than is found in many of the so-called softwood trees.

Another classification is based on whether the wood has open or closed grain. This is determined by the size of the wood pores and makes a difference in finishing procedures.

Some of the best kinds of wood for your work in the school shop are listed below. They are all hardwoods, except white pine, red cedar and redwood. Here they are grouped according to their actual hardness.

HARD	MED. HARD	SOFT
*Walnut	*Mahogany	White Pine
*Ash	*Limba	Basswood
Birch	*Butternut	Poplar
Cherry	*Chestnut	Willow
*Oak	Gum (red)	Red Cedar
Maple	*Elm (northern)	Redwood
	*Open grained wood.	

The grade of lumber depends on the size of the pieces and the defects (knots, stains, checks) it contains. The best grade of hardwood lumber is first and seconds (FAS) and contains about 90 percent clear cuttings. The next lower grade is selects (sometimes called FAS 1 face) which permits smaller pieces and more defects in the second or back face (surface). The lowest grade is No. 1 common and contains about 60 percent clear cuttings.

Softwood lumber (Fir, Pine, Spruce, Redwood, etc.) handled at local lumber yards is divided into a select and common classification. Select grades range from A through D with a B, or better, the highest grade usually available. Select grades are desirable for project work. The usual grades of common lumber range from No. 1 to No. 3 and are used for house framing and other rough carpentry.

Fig. 2-1. Left. Rough lumber. Center. Surfaced 2 sides. Right. Surfaced 4 sides.

The quality of lumber is also indicated by the method of drying. Air dried (AD) lumber is simply exposed to the air over a period of time. Kiln dried (KD) lumber is dried in huge ovens where temperature and humidity are carefully controlled. Kiln dried lumber usually has a lower moisture content and is free of internal stresses that are usually present in air dried lumber. Lumber that is to be used for cabinetwork and furniture should be kiln dried.

SURFACE AND SIZE

Hardwoods can be purchased either rough (Rgh.) or surfaced on both sides (S2S), Fig. 2-1. Some of the wood is removed in the planing or surfacing operation so that a 1 in. hardwood board will actually measure 13/16 in. Hardwood lumber is usually not planed on the edges and is sold in random widths and lengths with only the minimum sizes specified.

Softwoods are surfaced on all faces and edges (S4S) and are sold in specified widths from 2 to 12 in. by 2 in. intervals and in lengths of 8 to 20 ft. by 2 ft. intervals. A 1 x 4 will actually measure 3/4 x 3 1/2 in. The width of (S4S) lumber is reduced by 1/2 in. for pieces 6 in. and under. Over 6 in. the reduction is 3/4 in.

Lumber is always listed and sold according to its nominal (name) size. This is the size of the stock when it was "in the rough." It will be good practice for you to use this nominal size as you list and work with stock in the school shop.

ROUGH AND FINISHED SIZES

SOFTWOODS		HARDWOODS	
RGH. (NAME SIZE)	S4S	RGH. (NAME SIZE)	S2S
1 x 2	3/4 x 1 1/2	1/2	5/16
1 x 4	3/4 x 3 1/2	5/8	7/16
1 x 6	3/4 x 5 1/2	3/4	9/16
2 x 4	1 1/2 x 3 1/2	1	13/16
2 x 6	1 1/2 x 5 1/2	1 1/2	1 5/16
2 x 8	1 1/2 x 7 1/4	2	1 3/4

PLYWOOD

Plywood is available in nearly all of the hardwoods. Fir plywood is the most common of the softwoods. Thicknesses of 1/8 in. to more than 1 in. are made with the more common sizes including 1/4, 3/8, 1/2 and 3/4 in. A standard panel size is 4 ft. wide by 8 ft. long, however, many smaller sizes are offered for sale, especially in the hardwoods. Plywood is constructed of an odd number of ply — 3, 5, 7 — with the direction of the grain reversed in each successive layer. The outside layers are called face, and the inside layers are called the core. The best hardwood plywood is constructed with a thick solid stock for a core (called a lumber core), Fig. 2-2.

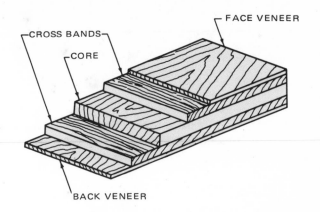

Fig. 2-2. Plywood construction.

In general the grade of plywood is determined by the quality of the face veneers. Hardwood plywood may be of good quality on both sides (G2S) or of good quality on only one side (G1S). The grade of a face varies with the quality of the veneer and the way it is cut and matched. The face veneer grades of softwood plywood range from A through D. The best piece of softwood plywood available would be an AA grade.

FIGURING BOARD FOOTAGE

Lumber is sold by the board foot. This is a piece that is 1 in. thick and 12 in. square (144 cu. in.). To figure the number of board feet in stock the following formula is used.

$$BF = \frac{No.\ Pcs.\ x\ T\ x\ W\ x\ L}{1\ x\ 12\ x\ 12}$$

For an example: find the number of board feet in 2 pcs. of wood that are 1 x 8 x 48.

$$BF = \frac{2\ x\ 1\ x\ \overset{2}{\cancel{8}}\ x\ \overset{4}{\cancel{48}}}{1\ x\ \underset{3}{\cancel{12}}\ x\ \underset{1}{\cancel{12}}} = \frac{16}{3} = 5\ 1/3$$

Stock that is less than 1 in. thick is figured as though it were 1 in. When the stock is thicker than 1 in. the nominal size is used. When the thickness is over one inch and includes a fraction such as 1 1/2, change it to an improper fraction (3/2) and place the numerator above the line and the denominator below the line. Example: find the board footage in one piece of stock, 1 1/2 x 10 x 36.

$$BF = \frac{\overset{1}{1} \times \overset{5}{3} \times \overset{3}{10} \times 36}{\underset{1}{2} \times 1 \times \underset{4}{12} \times \underset{1}{12}} = \frac{15}{4} = 3\ 3/4$$

Always use the nominal size of lumber to figure board footage. If the stock is long and the length is given in feet then one of the twelves (12s) can be dropped from the lower half of the formula.

Plywood is sold by the square foot in standard size panels. Prices vary for different thicknesses, kinds and grades.

SELECTING AND LAYING OUT

After you have made a stock-cutting list you are ready to look over the lumber stock and select a piece for your project. This requires good judgment. You may need the help of your instructor.

Look the stock over carefully on both sides and make a rough layout of the pieces you need, using a bench rule or a template, Fig. 2-3. White chalk works well since it is easily wiped off if you want to try other arrangements, Fig. 2-4. These will not be used for finished cutting but only to help you see how the piece will be cut up after it has been planed.

Be sure to look at the end of the stock. If the end is rough as it came from the sawmill, it will have small splits and checks that must be trimmed. It's very poor economy to cut stock and then find later that it contains defects that interfere with its use.

Fig. 2-4. Using chalk to make rough layout.

Some wood defects can be covered or placed on the back of your project. Very tight knots may even be desirable because of the beautiful grain patterns that are present around them.

Check your layout carefully to see that you have allowed: 1/16 in. thickness for planing, about 1/4 in. for each width you must cut out and about 1/2 to 1 in. for each length. Be sure the grain is running in the right direction in each piece. Use the framing square to mark a line across the stock as shown in Fig. 2-4.

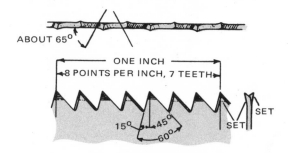

Fig. 2-5. Crosscut saw teeth.
(Stanley Tools)

Fig. 2-3. Using template to determine size of rough cutting.

Fig. 2-6. How the teeth of a saw cut.
(H. K. Porter Co.)

SAMMY SAFETY
SAYS:

"When starting the saw cut, keep your thumb high on the blade so if the saw should jump out of the kerf you will not cut yourself."

CUTTING STOCK TO ROUGH LENGTH

Select a crosscut saw that has 8 to 10 points per inch. Fig. 2-5 shows the shape of crosscut saw teeth. The set causes the saw to cut a "kerf" that is wider than the thickness of the blade, thus permitting it to move freely through the work, Fig. 2-6.

Support stock either in a bench vise or on sawhorses. Hold the saw in your right hand (if you are right handed) and place your left hand on the board, using your thumb as a guide to start the saw blade. Start the cut by pulling the saw toward you several times.

As soon as the saw is started, move your left hand away from the blade and hold the saw at about a 45 deg. angle, as shown in Fig. 2-7. If the saw starts to cut away from the line you can bring it back by twisting the blade slightly. Use long full strokes, feeding the saw into the cut with a slight pressure. Slow down as you near the end of the cut and support the wood so you will not split the corner. Be careful not to cut into the sawhorses or bench.

Plywood should be laid out and cut very carefully. It is best to make a scaled layout on paper if the parts are complicated. Lay out only the cutting lines since a plywood surface is already sanded and nearly ready for finish. Use a fine-tooth crosscut saw for all the cutting. Try to avoid splintering along the underside of the kerf.

RIPPING STOCK TO ROUGH WIDTH

If a piece is small, a crosscut saw can be used to rip it to width. A ripsaw which has chisel-shaped teeth will rip stock much faster than a crosscut saw and should be used on larger jobs.

Use the same general procedure for cutting with a ripsaw as described for the crosscut saw. The ripsaw works best when it is held at a 60 deg. angle with the surface of the work. A ripsaw should not be used for cutting plywood. Refer to Figs. 2-8 and 2-9.

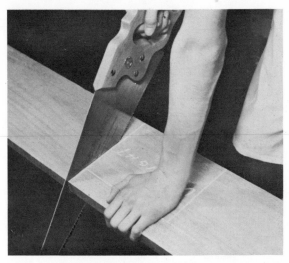

Fig. 2-7. Cutting stock to rough length.

Fig. 2-8. Trimming on end with the stock clamped between the vise dog and bench stop.

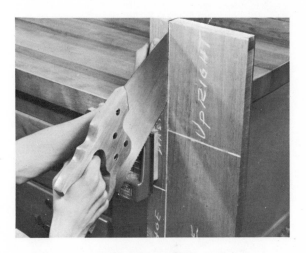

Fig. 2-9. Ripping to rough width with the stock clamped in a vise.

QUIZ – UNIT 2

1. Softwood trees are often called _____ because many of the trees in this classification bear cones.
2. The second best grade of hardwood lumber is called _____ .
3. The third best grade of hardwood lumber is called No. 1 Common and contains about _____ percent clear cuttings.
4. Softwood lumber that is handled by local lumber yards is divided into a select grade and a _____ _____ grade.
5. One inch hardwood lumber is surfaced (S2S) to a thickness of _____ .

6. A piece of 2 x 6 fir would actually measure 1 1/2 in. by _____ in.
7. When hardwood plywood is good on both faces the symbol _____ is used in the description.
8. The grade of the faces of softwood plywood are indicated by the letters A through _____ .
9. There are _____ board feet in a piece of lumber 1 in. x 9 in. x 54 in.
10. There are _____ board feet in a piece of lumber that is 1/2 in. x 8 in. x 5 ft.
11. If 1 1/2 in. walnut is selling for 60 cents a board foot, a piece 4 in. x 36 in. will cost _____ .

Drying and sorting veneer in modern plywood manufacturing. Infeed end of huge dryer is over 100 ft. long. Automatic mechanism distributes individual sheets to one of several conveyor levels. Carefully controlled temperatures (up to 360 deg. F.) and air movement reduce the MC (moisture content) to the desired level in about 10 minutes. (Georgia-Pacific Corp.)

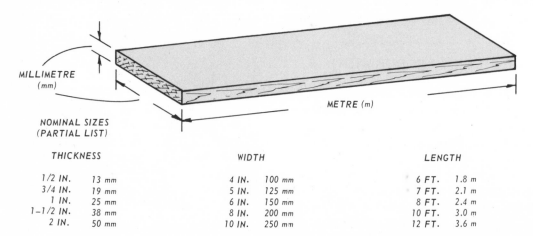

MILLIMETRE (mm)

METRE (m)

NOMINAL SIZES (PARTIAL LIST)

THICKNESS		WIDTH		LENGTH	
1/2 IN.	13 mm	4 IN.	100 mm	6 FT.	1.8 m
3/4 IN.	19 mm	5 IN.	125 mm	7 FT.	2.1 m
1 IN.	25 mm	6 IN.	150 mm	8 FT.	2.4 m
1-1/2 IN.	38 mm	8 IN.	200 mm	10 FT.	3.0 m
2 IN.	50 mm	10 IN.	250 mm	12 FT.	3.6 m

Standard lumber sizes in U.S. Customary and SI metric (also see pages 116 and 117).

PLANING AND SAWING STOCK TO FINISHED DIMENSIONS

UNIT 3

1. **How to sharpen and adjust a plane.**

2. **How to use the plane on surfaces and edges.**

3. **How to cut stock to finished length with a backsaw.**

THE PLANE AND ITS PARTS

If you examine a catalog of hand tools you will find many types and sizes of planes. This list would include such names as Smooth, Jack, Fore, Jointer, Block, Rabbet, Circular, Router and Model Builders. For your work in squaring up stock you should use a smooth plane and/or a jack plane and a block plane. A smooth plane is shown in Fig. 3-1. It is usually 8 or 9 in. long. The jack plane is the same type but larger, ranging in length from 11 1/2 to 15 in. The standard model is 14 in. long and has a 2 in. cutter.

forming of the cutting edge and bevel. Honing involves work on only the cutting edge to make it "razor" sharp. An edge tool can usually be honed a number of times before it requires grinding.

Apply a few drops of oil to the face of an oilstone and place the bevel of the plane iron flat on the surface. Now raise the end slightly so that just the cutting edge rests on the stone. Maintain this angle and move the plane iron forward and backward over the surface of the stone, as shown in A, Fig. 3-2.

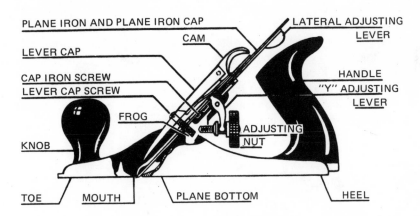

Fig. 3-1. Parts of a standard plane.

The plane is a tool with which you should become well acquanited. Take your plane apart and study it along with Fig. 3-1, so that you will know the name of its parts, and how they fit together.

HONING PLANE IRON

Sharpening a plane iron involves operations called grinding and honing. Grinding is the shaping and

Continue these strokes until you can feel a fine wire edge when you move your finger, lightly, across the top of the plane iron and out over the edge. Turn the plane iron over, lay it flat on the stone and stroke it a few times as shown in B, Fig. 3-2.

Turn the iron back to the bevel side and give it a few light strokes and then again stroke the top of the iron held flat on the stone. Repeat this several times

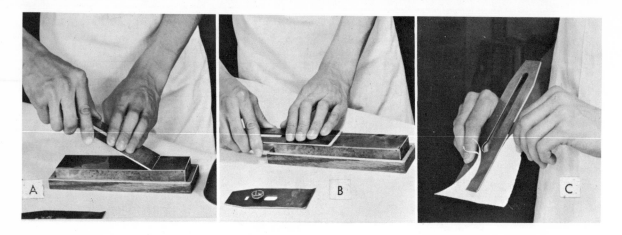

Fig. 3-2. Honing the plane iron.

until the wire edge has disappeared. The edge will now be sharp and "keen" and should cut a piece of paper as shown in C, Fig. 3-2.

When you finish with the oilstone, wipe the oil from the surface and replace the cover.

GRINDING A PLANE IRON

Fig. 3-3 shows the grinding of a plane iron held in a special attachment that makes it easy to form a perfect bevel. Position the iron carefully in the clamp so that the width of the bevel ground will be about two and one-third times the thickness of the plane iron. Move the iron back and forth across the revolving wheel until the edge is so thin that a burr starts to form. Grind just a little heavier on the outside corners so that the cutting edge will be about 1/32 in. higher in the center. Some woodworkers prefer to form this slight crown on an oilstone.

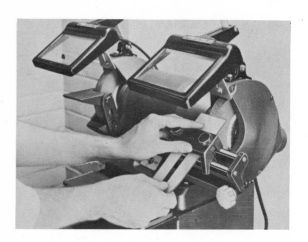

Fig. 3-3. Grinding a plane iron.   (Stanley Tools)

During the grinding, keep the plane iron cool by dipping it in water. If the grinder does not have an approved eye shield, you must wear goggles to protect your eyes.

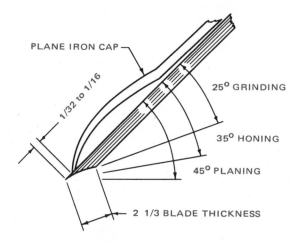

PLANE IRON CAP

1/32 to 1/16

25° GRINDING

35° HONING

45° PLANING

2 1/3 BLADE THICKNESS

Fig. 3-4. Double plane iron assembled.

ADJUSTING THE PLANE

Position iron cap on the plane iron as shown in Fig. 3-4 and tighten the cap iron screw. The edge of the plane iron cap must fit tight against the top of the plane iron, otherwise shavings will feed under it and prevent the plane from cutting properly.

Carefully place this assembly (often called a double plane iron) into the plane and secure its position with the lever cap. If necessary, adjust the setting of the lever cap screw so that the cam of the lever cap locks in place with a smooth firm pressure.

Turn the plane upside down and sight across the bottom, looking toward a window or other source of light. Turn the adjustment nut clockwise until the blade projects above the plane bed about 1/16 in. Now move the lateral adjustment lever from side to side until the cutting edge is parallel to the bottom face of the plane. Turn the adjustment nut counterclockwise until the cutting edge is withdrawn below the surface of the plane bottom. Place the plane on the surface of the stock and again turn the adjustment nut clockwise until the plane edge just begins to cut the stock.

PLANING A SURFACE

If you will look closely at the surface of some solid stock you will find there are very small "waves" (called mill marks) which were formed by the rotating knives of a power plane. Fig. 3-5. These should be removed with a hand plane. It takes a great amount of hand sanding to remove such marks, and since they are slightly compressed into the wood by the machine, there is a tendency for them to reappear when finish is applied. Hand planing will also remove warp and other imperfections in the surface of the stock. See Fig. 3-6.

Plane the best face of the stock first. By examining the edge of the board try to determine the direction of the grain and clamp the stock in position so that you will be planing with the grain. Most stock can be laid flat on a bench and clamped between a bench stop and vise dog.

Place the plane on the stock and move it over the surface, gradually turning the adjustment nut until a fine shaving is cut. You may find that the plane cuts in some spots and not in others. This indicates high places in the surface. Continue to plane these high spots until they disappear and the plane "takes" a shaving across the entire surface. Keep the plane set for a very fine cut. The shavings should be light and "feathery" and should seem to almost float when you drop a handful to the floor. Try to produce a smooth, true surface with as little planing as possible.

Generally, it is considered best to plane the surface of your stock while it is in one piece and before it is cut into smaller parts. If, however, there is much warpage present, you should cut the stock into smaller pieces before hand planing. Warped stock can be straightened by planing across or diagonally with the grain.

Fig. 3-5. Above. Mill marks on stock surfaced with a power plane. Below. Surface after hand planing.

Turn the stock end over end and plane the other side. Measure the stock at several points to determine finished thickness.

Fig. 3-6. Planing a surface with a smooth plane.

On some work the hand surfacing operation should be done later. If it is necessary to make edge joints to secure the required width of stock, then the hand surfacing operation should be left until after these joints have been made. In Fig. 3-7, the outside surfaces of the box are being planed, after the box was glued together.

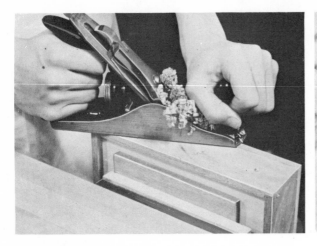

Fig. 3-7. Planing the sides of a box after assembly.

Fig. 3-9. Planing edge of assembled project.

PLANING AN EDGE

In Fig. 3-8 a jack plane is being used to plane the edge of the stock. Notice that one end is held in the vise, and the other is supported by a hand screw that rests on the bench surface. Select the best edge to plane first, since slight defects on the second edge may be removed when the stock is reduced to the required width. A smooth plane may be used to plane the edge; however, the longer bed of the jack plane will produce a straighter surface.

Fig. 3-8. Planing an edge with a jack plane.

In planing an edge, use the same suggestions as were made for planing a surface. Fig. 3-9. Continue to plane the edge until the plane will take one thin, continuous shaving the entire length of the board.

Use a try square to check the edge for squareness with the best face.

From the finished edge, lay out the required width and draw a line down the length of the stock. Turn the stock end over end and plane to the line. Some woodworkers prefer to square the ends to finished length before planing the second edge.

SQUARING END OF STOCK

You can secure an accurate end cut by following the procedure shown in Fig. 3-10. Clamp the straight edge firmly along the line to be cut. Tighten the outside spindle of the hand screw last since it provides the greatest leverage.

Place the blade of the backsaw against the straightedge and start the cut. With the left hand, apply pressure to the side of the saw so the blade will be held firmly against the straightedge throughout the cut. The teeth of a backsaw are small (14 points to the in.) and will not cut very fast. Use long steady strokes. Sawdust cut near the center of the board must be moved to the edge of the stock, before it can be cleared from the saw kerf. Short strokes will not clear the sawdust and it will work up along the sides of the saw and cause the blade to bind. Notice that the stock is clamped to a scrap piece that protects the saw from the vise and supports the wood fibers on the under side of the cut.

From the squared end lay out the finished length. Use the same procedure to cut off the second end. Whenever possible, clamp the straightedge on the

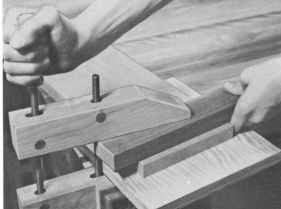

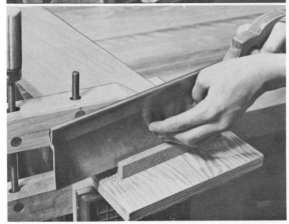

Fig. 3-10. Squaring end of stock. Above. Marking with a pencil and try square. Center. Clamping a straightedge along the line. Below. Making the cut with a backsaw.

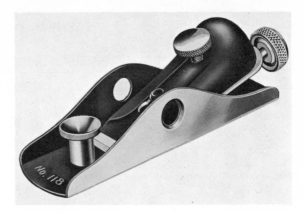

Fig. 3-11. A block plane.
(Stanley Tools)

In end planing, a block plane will do the best work, Fig. 3-11. In this plane, the blade sets at a low angle with the bevel side turned up. It makes a "shearing" type of cut. The block plane is designed to be held in one hand, leaving the other hand free to hold or support the work. It will do all kinds of small planing jobs, and is useful for trimming the edges of plywood.

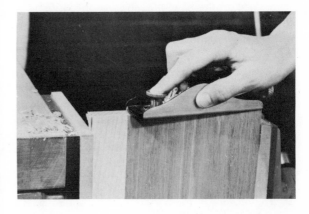

Fig. 3-12. Planing an end with the block plane. The waste stock (light wood) supports the edge, and prevents splitting.

stock so that the saw kerf will be on the "waste" side of the line. If you cannot do this, you will need to make an allowance for the width of the saw kerf.

PLANING END GRAIN

End grain is hard to plane. Because of this, it is usually worth while to give extra attention to saw cuts across the grain, so that they will be square and not require planing. End grain that will be exposed in the finished project should be planed.

When planing end grain, the cut should not carry over an edge or end unless the wood fibers are supported as shown in Fig. 3-12. When the board is wide it is easiest to plane in from each edge, toward the center. It is recommended to use a very light cut when planing end grain.

SQUARING SMALL PARTS

Small parts are often difficult to plane and saw. They are hard to clamp and hold and the regular tools seem large and "clumsy."

Fig. 3-13. Squaring small parts with the dovetail saw and a special jig.

construction problem. Industrial plants use many jigs and fixtures to provide speed and accuracy in their work.

Sanding should usually not be started until all tool operations are complete. Small parts, however, can be squared quickly and easily on the sanding board shown in Fig. 3-14. The straightedge must have faces and edges that are square with each other. Grip the block being squared close to the sandpaper surface, otherwise it will tend to tip over. The straightedge could be made at an angle to sand some special part.

Fig. 3-13 shows a jig that works well for sawing small parts. It clamps in the vise like a bench hook, and works in about the same way as a miter box. The dovetail saw being used has a thin blade, very fine teeth and makes a smooth cut. A regular backsaw will also work satisfactorily. When constructing the jig, the block that guides the saw is cut in two pieces and then glued to the base with the saw in position. A little paste wax, applied to this "kerf" or slot will make the saw run smoothly.

Jigs like this are not difficult to build and will help you do a better job. You may want to "try your hand" at designing some kind of a jig for some special

Fig. 3-14. Using a sanding board and a straightedge to square a small piece.

QUIZ — UNIT 3

1. A _____ plane is about 8 or 9 in. long.
2. The opening in the bottom of the plane through which the plane iron extends is called the _____ .
3. The double plane iron assembly is held in the plane with the _____ .
4. A right-handed worker holds the _____ of the jack or smooth plane in his left hand.
5. A plane iron should usually be sharpened so that the edge is about _____ higher in the center.
6. The width of the bevel ground on the plane iron should be about _____ times the thickness of the blade.
7. To increase the depth of cut of a jack plane, the _____ _____ is turned clockwise.
8. The small waves left on a wood surface by the power planer are called _____ .
9. To line up the edge of the plane iron with the surface of the plane bottom, the _____ adjustment is moved.
10. Sharpening operations for an edge tool include grinding and _____ .
11. To secure the greatest pressure from a hand screw the _____ spindle should be tightened last.
12. The backsaw has teeth which are small and number about _____ points to the inch.

MAKING WOOD JOINTS

UNIT 4

1. Some of the common types of wood joints.
2. How to lay out and plane an edge joint.
3. How to use a straightedge and jig to cut rabbet and dado joints.

There are a great many kinds of joints used to connect wood parts. Some of the basic types are shown in Fig. 4-1. Most wood joints are held together with glue. Strength of the joints depends on the amount of contact area (the surface of one piece touching the other piece) and the quality of the glue job. Joints that do not have much contact area are usually reinforced with nails, screws, dowels or other fastening devices.

The pieces to be joined should first be squared and cut to size. For some joints you will need to allow extra stock to form the joint. Lay out the cuts carefully, using a sharp pencil or knife. When possible, it is good practice to mark one piece by holding the second piece over it and in the correct position. Lay out all the same kind of joints at one time. Sometimes this is done by clamping identical pieces together. Identify the two members of a given joint with a number or letter so that they can be easily matched during assembly.

BUTT AND EDGE JOINTS

A butt joint that is held together with glue is not very strong and should be reinforced with dowels, nails or screws. Usually it is best to clamp the parts of a butt joint together, while driving nails or setting screws. A doweling jig can be used to position and guide the bit when drilling holes for dowels.

The edge joint holds securely with glue but can be reinforced with dowels or splines. It is used to join narrow pieces to form wider widths. Lay out the pieces to be joined so the grain is matched, and runs in the same direction. The annular ring pattern should be reversed in every other piece as shown in Fig. 4-2. After the position of the pieces has been determined, make reference marks on the top surface.

Planing an edge joint (Fig. 4-3) requires careful work. Clamp two adjacent pieces together in a vise with the top surfaces (marked) turned to the outside.

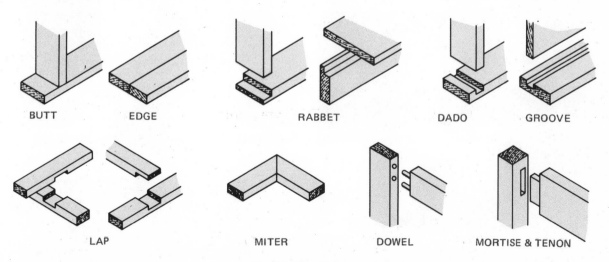

BUTT   EDGE   RABBET   DADO   GROOVE

LAP   MITER   DOWEL   MORTISE & TENON

Fig. 4-1. Wood joints.

Fig. 4-2. Selecting and marking edge joints. Notice that the grain pattern has been matched and the annular rings are reversed in adjoining pieces.

Plane the edges until you are able to take a light, thin shaving along the entire length. Remove the pieces from the vise and place them together to check the fit. Slight variations in the joint can now be corrected by planing each piece separately. Have your instructor check the joint. Next, refer to Unit number 7 for suggestions on gluing the pieces together.

To install dowels in the edge joint, clamp the two pieces in the vise (top surfaces on the outside) with the edges and ends even. Square lines across the edge where each dowel will be located. Dowels should be spaced about 4 to 6 in. apart. The diameter of the dowel should be equal to one half the thickness of the stock.

A doweling jig (Fig. 4-5) makes it easy to bore the holes. Mount a bit guide of the correct diameter in

the jig and position the holder so it is in the center of the stock. Place a depth gage on the bit to provide a hole 1/16 in. deeper than half of the dowel length. In a dowel joint the dowels should enter each piece of wood a distance equal to about two and one half times their diameter.

Line up the jig with the layout mark, clamp it securely and bore the hole. Turn the jig around so the fence is on the other side, align with the mark and bore the matching hole. Follow the same procedure and bore all the other holes before removing the pieces from the vise.

Fig. 4-4. Installing dowels in an edge joint. Above. Laying out the position of the dowels. Below. Boring holes with the doweling jig.

Fig. 4-3. Planing an edge joint. Both pieces are clamped in the vise with the top faces turned to the outside.

The edges of flooring and siding are joined with a tongue and groove or lap joint. In production

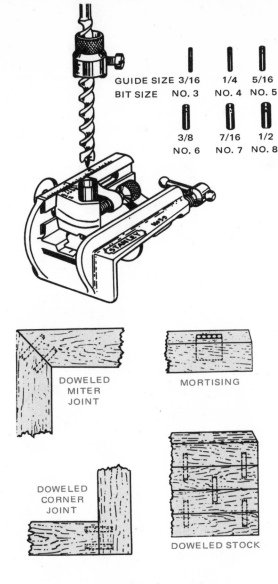

GUIDE SIZE 3/16   1/4   5/16
BIT SIZE   NO. 3   NO. 4   NO. 5

3/8   7/16   1/2
NO. 6   NO. 7   NO. 8

DOWELED MITER JOINT

MORTISING

DOWELED CORNER JOINT

DOWELED STOCK

Fig. 4-5. A doweling jig and doweled joints.
(Stanley Tools)

woodwork, edges that will be glued together are often cut with a multiple tongue and groove.

RABBET JOINTS

The rabbet joint is made by cutting a recess in one of the pieces to be joined. It may be cut along the edge or on the end of the stock, and is a good joint for mounting panels in frames or joining corners in box construction. The width of a rabbet joint is equal to the thickness of the mating part and the depth should be about two thirds of the thickness of the stock being cut. When working with plywood a greater depth is often used so very little of the edge of the plywood will show in the assembled joint.

The jig shown in Fig. 4-6 will help you make an accurate cheek (end grain) cut. A thin strip (thickness determined by the size of the joint) is glued to a piece of flat stock. Clamp the jig in the vise and then clamp the work to the jig with a hand screw. The backsaw is held firmly against the jig while the cut is being made.

Fig. 4-6. Cutting a rabbet joint. Above. Using a jig to lay out the joint. Center. Clamping the stock to the jig. Below. Making the cheek cut with the backsaw.

The shoulder cut is made by clamping a straightedge along the line, in the same manner as was suggested for squaring the end of stock. You can check your layout by placing the mating pieces against the straightedge and checking to see if it lines up with the end of the stock being cut. Use a wood chisel to trim or straighten the surfaces of the joint.

When cutting a rabbet along the edge of stock it is best to use a rabbet plane as shown in Fig. 4-7. This plane has an adjustable fence and depth gage that controls the width and depth of cut. Adjust the controls of the plane and practice cutting a rabbet in a piece of scrap lumber before using it on your work.

Fig. 4-7. Using a rabbet plane to cut a joint with the grain.

DADOS AND GROOVES

A dado is a rectangular recess cut in the wood and running across the wood grain. A groove is the same type of cut but runs along the grain of the wood. Both the dado and the groove are cut to a depth equal to one half the thickness of the stock.

Lay out the dado on the face and edges of the stock. Clamp a straightedge along one of the lines so that the kerf will be on the waste side and then make a cut to the proper depth with a backsaw. Move the straightedge to the other line and clamp it lightly. Place the part that will fit into the dado (mating part) against the straightedge and align its surface with the outside edge of the first saw cut. If you make this adjustment carefully you will get a perfect fit. Now clamp the straightedge securely, remove the mating part and make the second cut. On wide boards, use

long strokes, so that the saw dust that is cut in the center of the piece, will be carried to the edge and removed from the saw kerf.

Use a chisel to remove the waste wood between the saw kerfs. The straightedge should be left in

Fig. 4-8. Cutting a dado joint. Above. Setting the straightedge for the second saw cut. Center. Making the second cut with the backsaw. Below. Using a 3/4 in. chisel to remove the waste stock.

place, since it will serve as a guide for the chisel as shown in Fig. 4-8. Rough cuts should be made with the bevel of the chisel turned down or against the wood. For fine, finished cuts this position is reversed.

The dado can be finished with a router plane as shown in Fig. 4-9. This will make the bottom of the dado level and true. Make the cuts in from each side toward the center to prevent splitting the edges of the joint.

Fig. 4-9. Finishing dado joint with router plane.

Grooves are cut in about the same way as dados. The marking gage can be used to lay out the groove and is especially helpful on long pieces. Use a straightedge to guide the saw when cutting the sides of the groove. The panel or mating part will help to position the straightedge for the second cut.

Use a chisel that is about the same width as the groove to remove the wood from between the saw kerfs. A router plane can be used to finish the bottom of the groove.

The final trimming and fitting of grooves and dados can be done with a chisel. Lay the chisel flat on the work with the bevel turned out when making light, paring cuts. If the joint is too tight it is often easier to plane off the necessary thickness of the mating piece than to enlarge the width of the dado or groove. See Fig. 4-10.

LAP JOINTS

In the lap joint an equal amount of wood is removed from each piece. There are a number of

different types of lap joints with such names as end lap, half lap, edge lap, and the cross lap and middle lap as shown in Fig. 4-1.

Lap joints are easy to lay out, using a try square and a marking gage. Or, you can lap the two pieces to be joined and, along the edge of each piece, mark lines on the face of the other piece.

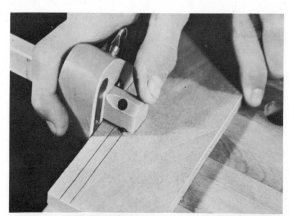

Fig. 4-10. Cutting a groove. Above. Using a marking gage for the layout. Center. Making the second cut with the backsaw. Below. Using a 1/4 in. chisel to remove waste stock.

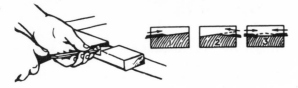

Fig. 4-11. Using the chisel to remove waste stock from a lap joint.

Use the same procedures for sawing and removing the waste stock as was described for cutting the rabbet and dado joints, Fig. 4-11. If the joint is very wide, it may be helpful to make several saw cuts in the waste stock. When the joint fits too tight, it may be easier to reduce the width of the pieces, rather than to trim the shoulder cuts.

MITER JOINTS

The miter joint is formed by cutting an equal angle (usually 45 deg.) on each of the mating parts. It is an attractive joint since none of the end grain of the parts is visible. The miter joint does not have much strength and is often reinforced with wood or metal splines or dowels.

The miter box shown in Fig. 4-12 is designed especially for cutting angles. Swing the saw carrier to the 45 deg. position, and hold the stock firmly on the bed and against the back. For very accurate work, the stock should be clamped in position, either with a hand screw or special clamps provided on some miter boxes. Use long steady strokes while making the cut. The weight of the saw will be sufficient to feed it into the work. On small pieces it may be necessary to "hold up" on the saw so that it will not cut too fast.

MORTISE-AND-TENON JOINTS

The mortise-and-tenon joint is very strong, and is used in the construction of quality furniture and cabinetwork. Making this joint by hand requires considerable skill. You should not attempt it until you have had successful experience making some of the other joints described in this section.

Study a number of good working drawings showing mortise-and-tenon joints, before designing and laying out your own. The thickness of the tenon is usually one half the thickness of the stock but other dimensions may vary widely depending on how the joint is used. When laying out several joints it is best to clamp similar pieces together and square lines across all of them at the same time.

The mortise is cut first by boring a series of holes within the layout lines. A doweling jig will be helpful

Fig. 4-12. Using a miter box.

in this operation. A chisel is used to remove the remaining waste stock and to trim the corners and sides.

Check the size of the tenon layout against the mortise that has been cut, and adjust if necessary. Use a jig to make the cheek cuts (similar to the one used for the rabbet joint). When all of the cheek cuts are complete, make the shoulder cuts by clamping a straightedge along the line to be cut. If you are making a number of joints, you may want to design a special jig to speed up your work on these cuts.

When you select a joint that is hard to make, like the mortise-and-tenon joint, you should make a sample joint out of scrap wood before making the joints for your project.

QUIZ – UNIT 4

1. The layout lines of a joint can be made with a pencil or_____ .
2. A butt joint is usually held together with dowels, nails or_____ .
3. When making edge joints to form a wide board it is important that the_____ _____ be reversed in every other piece.
4. The diameter of the dowels installed in an edge joint should be equal to_____ the thickness of the stock.
5. The hole for a dowel should be drilled about _____ in. deeper than the dowel length will require.
6. The depth of a rabbet cut in 3/4 in. stock should be about _____ .
7. The depth of a dado cut in 5/8 in. stock should be _____ .
8. When laying out a groove in a long piece it is best to use a_____ .
9. The bottom of a dado joint can be leveled and finished with a_____ .
10. When making a mortise and tenon joint the _____ should be made first.

FORMING CURVES, CHAMFERS, BEVELS

1. **How to lay out curves and make patterns and templates.**
2. **How to cut irregular shapes and smooth the edges.**
3. **How to lay out and cut chamfers, bevels and tapers.**

Many articles made of wood contain curves and irregular shapes. The layout for some of these can be made directly on the wood, while for others it is necessary to develop a pattern and then transfer it to the wood.

The surface of solid stock should be hand planed before laying out and cutting irregular shapes. Since curved pieces are hard to clamp and hold, it is advisable to make joints and bore holes before cutting out the curved parts. Pieces that have only one or two curved edges should be squared to finished size with the saw and plane, before the curved edges are cut.

CIRCLES AND ARCS

Circles and arcs (part of a circle) can usually be laid out directly on the work using dividers or pencil compass. For large circles you can use the trammel points or a pencil attached to a piece of string. See Fig. 5-1.

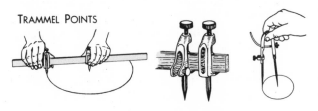

Fig. 5-1. Trammel points and dividers.

Set the dividers at one half the diameter of the circle, and place one leg at the center point. Tilt the dividers slightly in the direction of movement as you draw the circle; be sure to hold a piece of cardboard under the center leg for protection if it is located on a finished surface.

Using a compass, many geometric shapes can be developed. You probably have already had experience making a hexagon (6 sides) by laying off the radius of a circle around the circumference and connecting these points with a straight line.

CURVES

A smooth flowing curve is usually more interesting than a perfect circle or arc. These are the kind of curves that we see in the contour of airplanes, boats and automobiles. The engineer and draftsman call them "faired" lines. They are produced by drawing a smooth curve through a number of previously established points, using a long plastic spline (strip) held in place with special lead weights.

In the school shop small curves can be laid out with an irregular curve (sometimes called a French curve) which is usually included in the drafting equipment. A large curve can be laid out with a thin strip of wood in about the same way the draftsman uses a spline. It can be clamped to the wood for a single layout or used to develop a pattern.

To develop a pattern, fasten a sheet of paper to a piece of cork board or hardboard. Set large pins or small nails at the points you want the curve to pass through. Thread the wood strip through these points and draw a line along its edge, Fig. 5-2.

PATTERNS AND TEMPLATES

A pattern is a full-size outline of an object drawn on paper. Some patterns can be developed from dimensions given on a drawing. Complicated curves and outlines are included in working drawings but are usually not full size and need to be enlarged. This can

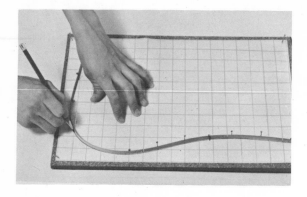

Fig. 5-2. Making a quarter pattern using a thin wood strip.

be easily done by a method called "enlarging with squares." Study the drafting book in this series for a complete description of the method. Basically, it is accomplished by laying out small squares (if not included on the drawing) over the contour to be enlarged. On a sheet of paper lay out larger squares (size depends on the scale or ratio), and number them to correspond with the squares on the drawing. Work with one square at a time and draw a line through the large square in the same way it goes through the corresponding small square.

When a design is the same on both ends, you need only a half pattern. This is laid out on one side of a center line, Fig. 5-3, and then turned over and laid out on the other side. Some designs require only a quarter pattern such as the one being used in Fig. 5-4.

You can transfer a pattern to wood by cutting it out and drawing around the edge or placing a piece of carbon paper between the pattern and the wood

surface and tracing over the lines. Secure the pattern to the work with drafting tape or thumb tacks so it will not slip. When tracing a pattern onto wood, use a straightedge and irregular curve to produce smooth lines on your work.

When you have a number of identical pieces to lay out it is usually best to make a template. Glue your paper pattern (use rubber cement) onto a heavy piece of cardboard or a thin piece of plywood or hardboard. Carefully cut out the design and then smooth the edges by filing and sanding.

CUTTING CURVES

A coping saw and a compass saw are hand tools used to cut curves. The coping saw has fine teeth (usually about 16 points or 15 teeth to the inch) and makes the smoothest cut.

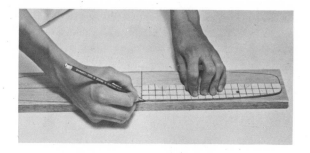

Fig. 5-4. Using a template to lay out a curve.

Coping saw work can be clamped in a vise, or held on a saw bracket or V support as shown in Fig. 5-5. When the work is held in a vise the blade should be mounted in the saw frame with the teeth pointing away from the handle. For work held on the saw bracket the teeth should point downward or toward the saw handle.

Start the cut in the waste stock and then guide the saw to the edge of the cutting line. Use steady, uniform strokes, keeping the blade perpendicular to the surface. Give the saw plenty of time to cut its way. Use extra strokes as you go around sharp corners. Reposition the work as you progress so the cutting will be taking place near the point of the V support or close to the jaws of the vise.

Working slowly (about 50 strokes a minute) and carefully will actually save time because you will not need to do as much filing or sanding to finish the

Fig. 5-3. Laying out center lines.

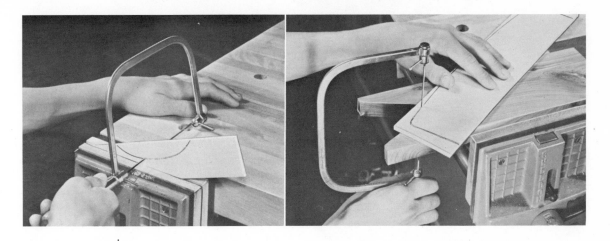

Fig. 5-5. Cutting with a coping saw. Left. Work being held in a vise. Right. Work being held on a V support.

edges. A new blade may "bite" into thin stock too fast for a smooth cut, and usually works better if it is given a few light strokes with a piece of fine sandpaper.

Curves that are formed by removing only a small amount of stock can be cut with a chisel. Inside curves are cut with the bevel held against the work and outside curves with the bevel turned out. Cut with the grain working toward the center of a curve as shown in Fig. 5-6.

SMOOTHING CURVES

The spokeshave is practical for smoothing and shaping a curved edge or surface. It is sharpened and adjusted somewhat like a plane. The spokeshave was originally designed to shape the wooden spokes of wagon wheels.

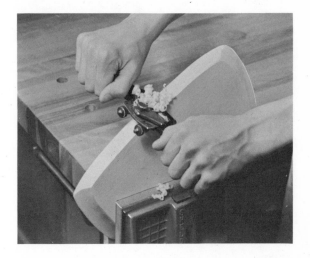

Fig. 5-7. Using a spokeshave.

Adjust the spokeshave and experiment with it on a piece of scrap wood. Mount your work in a vise. Hold the tool in both hands as shown in Fig. 5-7. It can either be pulled toward you or turned around and pushed. Take light cuts and work with the grain. Hold it at an angle with the work when cutting end grain.

For smoothing surfaces that are small or have sharp curves, it is best to use a wood file. The most common files for woodworking are the round, half-round and flat. Small metal files are sometimes helpful in smoothing intricate work. See Fig. 5-8.

When possible, use a stroking action rather than filing straight across an edge. Try to file in from each edge to prevent splitting the opposite side; this is

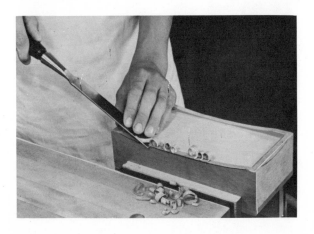

Fig. 5-6. Cutting a curved edge with a chisel.

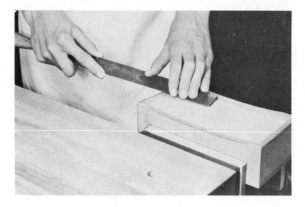

Fig. 5-8. Shaping an edge with a half-round file.

Fig. 5-9. Forming inside of tray with gouge.

especially inportant when working with plywood. Use a file card or file cleaner to keep the file teeth clean. A file should have a tight-fitting handle.

CARVING AND SHAPING

Gouges and chisels of various shapes are used for carving wood. They should be kept in a box or special holder when not being used, to protect the worker and also the cutting edges.

When carving wood, clamp the stock securely, either in a vise or in some special holder. Hold the tool in both hands and make cuts moving away from you. The angle of the tool edges will vary; however, most of them should be held at about a 30 deg. angle. Cut with the grain wherever possible.

Use a large outside-ground gouge to form the inside of a tray or boat hull. Start in the center and gradually enlarge the area. Cut long, thin shavings, with the tool moving toward the center as shown in

Fig. 5-9. Guide the blade with your left hand (if you are right handed) and force it through the wood with your right hand. Rolling the cutting edge slightly will help it cut, especially on end grain.

CHAMFERS AND BEVELS

A chamfer removes the sharp corner from an edge and improves the appearance of some work. It is usually made at a 45 deg. angle with the surface or edge of the stock.

Lay out a chamfer with a sharp pencil held so the fingers serve as a guide along the edge of the stock, as shown in Fig. 5-10. A marking gage cannot be used, since it will leave a groove.

Fig. 5-10. Laying out a chamfer.

Fig. 5-11. Planing a chamfer.

30

Clamp the stock in a hand screw and clamp the hand screw in a vise, so the work will be held at an angle. Plane the edges first, and then plane the ends with the plane held at an angle to make a shearing cut. See Fig. 5-11.

A bevel is a sloping edge that connects the two surfaces of the stock. It is laid out and cut in about the same manner as a chamfer. A sliding T-bevel should be set at the required angle and used to check the work.

SAMMY SAFETY
SAYS:

"When using a chisel always keep both hands back of the cutting edge with cutting motion away from you."

TAPERS

A taper runs along the length of stock causing it to be smaller at one end than the other. The legs of stools, chairs, and tables are often tapered.

First, square the stock to be tapered to its largest dimension. Lay out the length of the section to be tapered, mark the size of the small end and draw a line on each edge. Clamp the work in a vise and plane toward the tapered end.

For legs that are tapered on all four sides, first lay out and plane the taper on two opposite faces, as shown in Fig. 5-12. Mark the taper on these surfaces,

Fig. 5-12. Planing a taper.

and plane the remaining two sides. Tapers are hard to clamp in a vise and you may need to work out some special clamping arrangement.

QUIZ — UNIT 5

1. Before laying out and cutting curved pieces from solid stock, the surface of the stock should be _____ .
2. To lay out a large circle, use a set of _____ _____ or use a pencil and string.
3. When a full-sized outline of an object is drawn on paper it is called a _____ .
4. If your project contains a number of curved pieces that are the same size and shape, you should use a _____ to lay them out.
5. A standard coping saw blade has_____ points to the inch.
6. A tool that was originally designated to form wooden wheel spokes is called a _____ .
7. Three common shapes of wood files are flat, round and_____ .
8. Most chamfers are made at a _____ deg. angle with the surface or edge of the stock.
9. When planing a chamfer the work should be clamped so the plane can be held in a_____ position.
10. When planing a taper the cut should usually be made toward the _____ end.

Modern double-end tenoner. Feed chains (arrows) carry workpieces through saws and cutterheads — located on both sides. In the setup shown, drawer front blanks are first trimmed to exact length, rabbets are cut, and then the ends are shaped (see insert drawing). A special sanding attachment smooths the shaped surface as the pieces leave the machine. (Norton Co.)

DRILLING AND BORING HOLES

1. How to lay out hole positions.
2. How to use a brace and bit to bore holes.
3. How to bore holes at an angle.
4. How to use a hand drill.

Cutting small holes (1/4 in. dia. or less) in wood is called drilling. This operation is usually performed with a twist drill or drill press. Boring is the term used for cutting larger holes with the brace and auger bit or with a brad point bit mounted in a drill press.

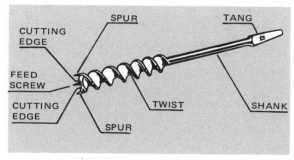

Fig. 6-2. Parts of an auger bit.

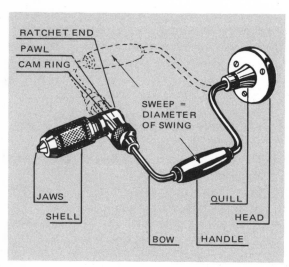

Fig. 6-1. Parts of a brace.
(Stanley Tools)

BRACES AND AUGER BITS

The size of a brace is determined by its "sweep," Fig. 6-1. Braces are available in sizes 8 to 14 in. A good size brace for a school shop is either 8 or 10 in. Most braces are equipped with a ratchet that permits boring in a corner even though a complete revolution of the handle cannot be made.

The most common types of wood bits are the double twist shown in Fig. 6-2, and the solid center. Fig. 6-5. A single twist is often used for boring deep holes because chips seldom clog in the spiral. There

are other types of boring tools especially designed for use on power equipment.

Auger bits are available in sizes ranging from a No. 3 through No. 32. This number is stamped on the tang of the bit and indicates the size in sixteenths of an inch. For example, a No. 5 would be 5/16 in. in diameter; a No. 12 would be 12/16 in. or 3/4 in. in diameter. A standard auger bit set is made up of numbers 4 through 16.

SHARPENING AN AUGER BIT

Sharpening an auger bit requires considerable skill and careful work. You should check with your instructor before attempting this operation.

A special auger bit file should be used to sharpen auger bits. Sharpen the cutters first by stroking upward through the throat as shown in Fig. 6-3. Use medium pressure and stop as soon as the edge is sharp. Try to maintain the original bevel. Turn the bit over and file the spurs on the inside surface only. Keep the bit balanced by filing the same amount on both sides.

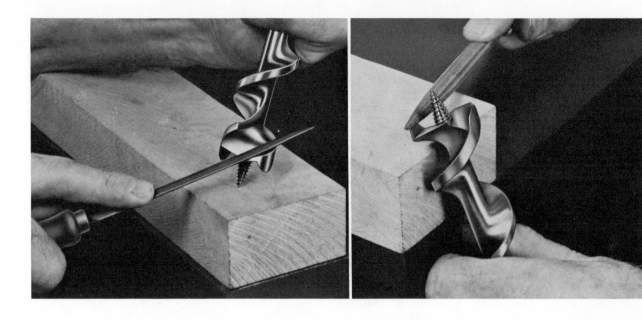

Fig. 6-3. Sharpening an auger bit.
(Greenlee Tool Co.)

The edges on an auger bit will stay sharp a long time if the bit is carefully handled. When not in use, keep auger bits in special holders, or in boxes or cloth rolls in which they were packed by manufacturer.

BORING A HOLE

Measure and lay out the position of the hole by drawing center lines on the best face of the stock. Punch a small hole with a sharp scratch awl where these lines intersect. Fig. 6-4.

The stock may be fastened in the vise in either a horizontal or a vertical position. It should be firmly clamped to a piece of waste stock that will support the wood around the edges of the hole when the bit cuts through the opposite side. When boring a large hole in a small piece of wood, prevent splitting by applying pressure to the sides with a hand screw.

Select the correct size bit and insert it well into the jaws of the brace. The corners of the tang are held in the Vs of the jaws. You can tighten or loosen the jaws by holding the shell and turning the brace handle.

Guide the bit with your left hand and set it in the hole marked with the awl. Turn the brace clockwise. Keep the bit perpendicular to the surface of the wood. Have another student help you "sight" this angle, or keep the bit aligned with a try square as shown in Fig. 6-5.

Fig. 6-4. Laying out center lines and center punching holes with a scratch awl.

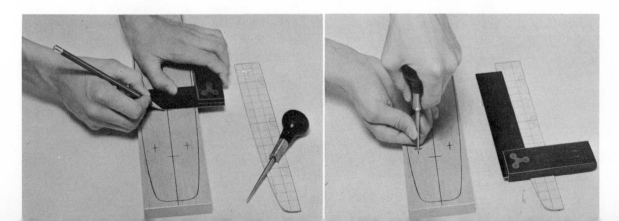

Fig. 6-5. Boring hole with brace and bit in vertical position. Notice the work is clamped to a piece of scrap wood.

It is usually easier to keep a bit perpendicular to the work when boring in a vertical position, but on some jobs it may be difficult to exert enough pressure. When an auger bit does not feed into the work properly, check the threads of the feed screw and see that they are clean.

Use extra care when starting a hole in plywood or you will splinter the veneer around the edge of the hole. Start the feed screw and turn the bit until the spurs just begin to score the outside of the hole. Turn the bit about a half turn backward, then forward,

Fig. 6-6. A spring-type bit depth gage.

several times, until the surface veneer is completely cut, before continuing to bore the hole.

If it is not convenient to "back up" the stock with scrap wood, you can bore from one side until the feed screw just starts to come through, then reverse the stock and finish the hole from the other side.

Hole depth may be regulated by using a depth gage, as shown in Fig. 6-6. An example of boring a hole with the brace and bit in a horizontal position is shown in Fig. 6-7.

COUNTERBORING

Sometimes it is necessary to have a hole of two different diameters. If you want to place a screw head below the surface of the work, you should first bore a hole for the head to the required depth and then make a hole with a drill that matches the size of the

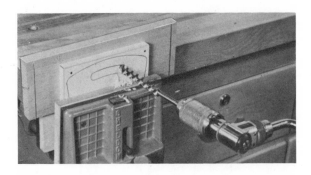

Fig. 6-7. Boring a hole with the brace and bit in a horizontal position.

shank of the screw. It is important that you bore the holes in this order. If the small hole is bored first there will be no way to center the larger bit.

BORING HOLES AT AN ANGLE

To bore a hole at an angle, set a sliding T-bevel at the required angle (use a protractor or the miter gage of the table saw) and place it on the surface to be bored. Start the feed screw and then tilt the bit to align with the blade of the T-bevel.

If you have several holes to bore at the same angle you can do more accurate work if you make a "boring jig" as shown in Fig. 6-8. It may be necessary for you to bore several holes before you get the angle you want. Place the jig on the bit and position the feed screw in the center punched hole. Start the feed screw by turning it about one turn. Tilt the bit and clamp the jig to the surface of the work. A piece of drafting or masking tape can be placed around the bit to serve as a depth gage.

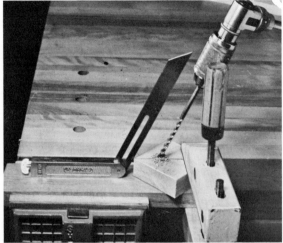

Fig. 6-8. Making and using a jig to bore holes at an angle. Above. Boring the jig. Center. The bit has been "threaded" through the jig and is being placed in the punched hole. Below. The jig has been clamped to the stock and the hole is being bored.

USING AN EXPANSIVE BIT

An expansive bit has adjustable cutters (usually two cutters) and will bore various size holes, Fig. 6-9.

Adjust the cutter so the distance from the spur to the center of the feed screw is equal to the radius of the hole. Some bits have a scale that will help you make this setting. After making the setting, lock the cutter securely. Start a test hole in a scrap block and measure it to check the setting before using it on your project.

It is better to bore through waste stock than to reverse the piece and finish the hole from the opposite side.

Fig. 6-9. Boring with an expansive bit.

USING A FORSTNER BIT

A Forstner bit does not have a feed screw and is used for boring holes that go only part way through the stock and require a smooth flat bottom. It can be used to enlarge holes or bore holes in thin stock where the feed screw of a regular bit might cause the stock to split. See Fig. 6-10. Locate position of holes to be bored with Forstner bit by drawing a circle or square the size of bit.

DRILLING HOLES

Holes 1/4 in. and smaller are usually drilled with a hand drill, using straight shanked twist drills. A push

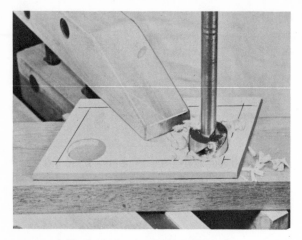

Fig. 6-10. Boring with a Forstner bit.

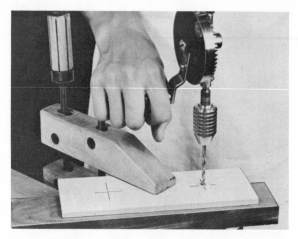

Fig. 6-12. Drilling a hole with a hand drill.

drill that required a special type of bit can be used for holes 1/16 in. to about 3/16 in. See Fig. 6-11. Carpenters quite often use a push drill to make holes for nails and screws. Such a drill can be operated with one hand.

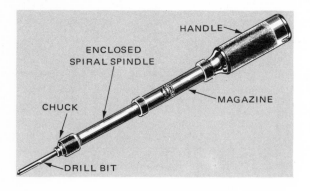

Fig. 6-11. Parts of push drill.

The size of a hand drill is determined by the capacity of its chuck (largest drill it will hold). The most common size for the school shop is 1/4 in. Twist drills are available in a wide range of sizes. For woodworking a good set should range from 1/16 to 1/4 in. by thirty-seconds.

In drilling holes, use the same procedure as suggested for boring holes. It is important that the hole be started with an awl since the twist drill has a blunt point. Place a twist drill all the way in the drill chuck. The jaws of the chuck may be opened and closed by holding the chuck and turning the handle.

Hold the handle in your left hand and keep the drill perpendicular to the wood surface, while turning the crank with your right hand. Small drills will break if you do not work carefully. Since there is no feed screw on a drill bit, you will control the feed by the pressure you apply. The amount of pressure to apply varies with the size of bit and the kind of wood. Drill to the required depth and continue to turn the drill while pulling it out of the hole. If the hole is deep, pull the drill out several times to clear the cuttings. Remove drill from chuck as soon as you have finished using it. See Fig. 6-12.

QUIZ — UNIT 6

1. The size of a brace is determined by the diameter of the handle swing or _____ .
2. The two most common types of auger bits are the double twist and the _____ _____ .
3. The number size of an auger bit is stamped on the _____ .
4. To bore a 3/8 in. hole, you should select a No. _____ auger bit.
5. A No. 8 auger bit will bore a hole that is _____ in. in diameter.
6. When sharpening an auger bit the spurs should be filed on the _____ surface.
7. Before boring a hole with the auger bit the center should be punched with a _____ _____ .

CLAMPING AND GLUING WOOD

UNIT 7

1. **Some of the kinds of glue used for woodwork.**

2. **How to make glue "spreads."**

3. **How to use wood clamps.**

WOOD GLUES

Research and developments in the last decade have produced many new adhesive products. The field of adhesives has become highly technical and complicated. We shall confine our study here to just a few adhesives that are most satisfactory for your work in the school shop.

POLYVINYL RESIN EMULSION GLUE (often referred to as white glue or just polyvinyl) has received wide acceptance. It comes ready for use in plastic squeeze bottles and is easily applied. This glue sets up rapidly, does not stain the wood or dull tools, and it holds wood parts securely.

Polyvinyl glue hardens when its moisture content is removed through absorption into the wood or through evaporation. Its "setting time" therefore depends somewhat on the porosity of the wood. It is not waterproof and should not be used in assemblies that will be subjected to high humidity or water. Polyvinyl does not resist high temperature (160F and higher) and should not be used in the construction of such articles as radio or TV cabinets. It never gets "brittle" hard and this characteristic makes it difficult to sand from a wood surface.

UREA-FORMALDEHYDE RESIN GLUE (usually referred to as urea resin) comes in a dry powder form. It is mixed with water to a creamy consistency for use. It is moisture-resistant, stains the wood only slightly and dries to a light brown color. It holds wood surfaces securely.

Urea resin hardens through chemical action in somewhat the same manner as portland cement. Elevated temperatures accelerate this action so if you

want to speed up the setting of your glue joints you may do so by placing them on a radiator or under a heat lamp. Wood is not a good conductor of heat; therefore, if the pieces are large it will take some time for the heat to penetrate to the "glue line."

This glue is well suited for use when gluing cutting boards, salad bowls, and articles that may be subjected to moisture for a short period of time.

RESORCINOL RESIN GLUE comes to the woodworker in two components; (1) a dark reddish liquid resin, and (2) a powdered or liquid hardener (sometimes called a catalyst). The components are mixed together for use. This glue has a "working life" of from two to four hours. Resorcinol glue has about the same working characteristics as urea resin. Its great advantage lies in its waterproof feature. It can be used with good results on boats, water skis or other structures exposed for long periods to high humidities or water.

TRY IT DRY — FIRST

Before applying any kind of glue you should place the parts together (trial assembly) and adjust the necessary clamps. Check the fit and squareness. All surfaces, especially inside ones, should be sanded before the final glue-up.

The wood surfaces that form the "glue line" should be dry, clean and free of sand dust and should make smooth contact with each other.

The joints should fit together without excessive pressure from clamps. If you force an assembly together you will be gluing stresses into your project that may eventually cause the joints or structural members to fail.

When using bar clamps on surfaces that are ready for finishing, it is important to use wood blocks under the clamp jaws to protect these surfaces from dents and stains.

MIXING POWDERED GLUES

Fig. 7-1 shows the mixing of urea resin glue. Since this glue has a working life of only two to three hours, you should mix just the amount needed for each job. A paper cup makes a good mixing container since it can be discarded when the job is finished.

Pour the dry powder into the cup and add a small amount of water. Stir with a stiff brush or stick until it forms a heavy "gooey" mass, then add a few drops of water at a time until you have reduced it to a smooth creamy consistency. Manufacturers of urea resin glue usually recommend a proportion (by measure) of eight parts of powder to three parts of water.

Be sure to close the container of powdered resin tightly, otherwise it will gather moisture from the air and harden in the container. If you use a brush to apply the glue it can be washed with warm water and soap.

Resorcinol glue should be handled in about the same manner as urea resin. Be sure to read the manufacturer's directions on the label. It is best to use sticks for mixing and application, since this type of glue is very difficult to remove from a brush.

MAKING THE GLUE SPREAD

Applying the glue to the wood surface is called "spreading." When the glue is applied to both wood surfaces to be joined it is called a "double spread" and when it is applied to only one surface it is called a "single spread."

Woodworking industries often use only a "single spread" since they have various devices and gluing machines that carefully control the amount of glue applied. For your work in the school shop it will be best to make a double spread (apply a coat of glue to both mating surfaces).

You must use good judgement as to how heavy to make the spread. The surface should be thoroughly coated, yet not so heavy that you will have excessive

Fig. 7-1. Mixing powdered glue.

"squeeze-out" for this will make the work messy and be wasteful of glue.

The time interval between coating the surfaces and bringing them together will vary with the type of glue used. When using polyvinyl you should close the assembly within two minutes. You will have about four minutes of "open assembly" time with urea resin at regular room temperatures and a much longer period with resorcinal resin.

Fig. 7-2 shows a sequence of gluing steps when working with polyvinyl. Notice that the double spread is made by rubbing the two pieces together. Where this spreading method is not practical, a stiff glue brush may be used. The brush should be cleaned in warm water immediately after use.

When spreading glue on a miter or butt joint the end grain of the wood will absorb extra glue. You can insure a good joint by making a second spread over these surfaces after the first spread has a few moments to soak in.

Since the "open assembly" time for polyvinyl is so short, you should plan to glue only a few parts of a complicated assembly at a time. This will not slow you down too much, since the glue sets rapidly.

CLEANING THE JOINT

On final assemblies, where the project surfaces have been sanded and are ready for finishing, it is important to keep them free of glue. Even the slightest amount of glue will seal the surface and cause a blemish in the final finished surface. Glue should be applied carefully so there is a minimum of "squeeze-out." That which does appear around the joint should be removed immediately and the surface "washed" with a sponge or rag rung out in hot water, Fig. 7-4.

Complete removal of the "squeeze-out" is not necessary when making edge or face joints. These joints are used to build wider or thicker stock and the excess glue is removed when it is worked to its

Fig. 7-3. Bar clamps holding edge joints.

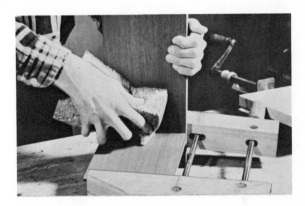

Fig. 7-4. Removing glue from the surface of the wood with a damp sponge.

finished dimension, Fig. 7-3. A wood scraper should be used to remove glue after it has hardened.

SETTING TIME

The setting time varies with the temperature of the glue line, the kind of wood, and the type of glue.

Polyvinyl takes an initial set in from 15 to 20 minutes. Most assemblies can be removed from the clamps after this period. Several hours, however, are required before it gains its full strength. Steel bar clamps that contact the glue line should not remain overnight as this will cause a stain in the wood.

Urea resin sets up more slowly. Projects should be left in clamps for several hours at room temperature.

Fig. 7-2. Gluing sequence using polyvinyl glue. Above. Applying from a "squeeze" bottle. Center. Making a "double spread." Below. Clamping with handscrew.

Fig. 7-5. This jig makes it easy to assemble miter joints.

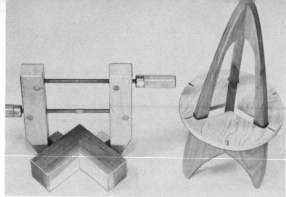

Fig. 7-6. Special clamping methods. Left. Small blocks are glued in place and then split off after the miter joint has been glued. Right. The plywood "yoke" for a tripod lamp applies pressure and holds the legs in proper position.

Either of these glues should cure over night before continuing to work with the material. This is especially true of polyvinyl as it gives the moisture absorbed from the glue line time to disperse through the wood and evaporate.

SIZES OF WOOD CLAMPS

Bar clamps, the type of clamps shown in Fig. 7-3, vary in size from two to eight feet. This size applies to the largest actual opening obtainable between the jaws.

The handscrews shown in Fig. 7-2 are sized by numbers ranging from 5/0 to 7. The 5/0 is the smallest and has a jaw 4 in. long. The next size is a 4/0 and has a 5 in. jaw. The largest size (Number 7) has a jaw length of 24 in.

Some of your assemblies may not be adaptable to regular wood clamps, and you will need to design special holders or jigs. This is comparable to work in industry. When new parts are designed, it is usually necessary to develop special tools, jigs and fixtures to provide speed and accuracy. Note Figs. 7-5, 7-6.

QUIZ – UNIT 7

1. Polyvinyl resin glue is a type of glue that hardens when its _____ content is removed.
2. The greatest disadvantage of polyvinyl resin glue is that it is not _____ .
3. Urea resin glue must be mixed with _____ before it is used.
4. Urea resin hardens due to chemical action and becomes a light _____ color.
5. It is possible to speed up the setting time of urea resin glue by raising the _____ of the glue line.

6. A glue designed for wood that is classified as being completely waterproof is called _____ resin.
7. Some resin glues are designed to set up when a catalyst or _____ is added to them.
8. When the parts of a project are fitted together before applying glue it is called a _____ _____ .
9. When using bar clamps to hold an assembly you should protect surfaces that are ready for finish by using _____ .
10. When glue is applied to both of the wood surfaces being joined it is called a _____ _____ .
11. The open assembly time when working with polyvinyl glue should not be over _____ minutes.
12. The open assembly time for urea resin is _____ minutes.
13. A second spread of glue should be made on the end grain of butt and _____ joints.
14. Urea resin glue is usually mixed to proportion (by measure) of 8 to _____ .
15. Excess glue that has hardened on edge joints should be removed with the _____ .
16. In addition to the type of glue and temperature of the glue line the setting time will vary somewhat depending on the kind of _____ .
17. Joints glued with polyvinyl can usually be removed from the clamps in about _____ minutes.
18. When gluing up stock for cutting boards the most practical glue to use is _____ _____ .
19. Standard bar clamps vary in size from two to _____ feet.
20. The number size of handscrews is determined by the length of the _____ .

METAL FASTENERS FOR WOODWORK

1. **How to drive nails.**

2. **Kinds and sizes of nails and screws.**

3. **How to use wood screws to assemble wood parts.**

HAMMERS AND NAILS

You probably have already had some experience driving nails. Nevertheless you should check Fig. 8-1 to be sure that you know the correct procedure. Notice where the hand grips the hammer. Center lines through the nail and hammer handle should form a right angle when the hammer face strikes the head of the nail.

Start the nail with light strokes, then get the hand that held the nail well out of the way. Use a fairly full swing (depending on the size of the nail) to get power in the stroke. Keep your eyes on the nail head — just like you would do when hitting a baseball or golf ball. Ease up on the power of your stroke when the head gets close to the surface of the wood, and stop when the head is flush. Do not "batter-up" the surface of the wood. Hammer marks are the trade marks of an ameteur.

Brads, finishing nails and casing nails are used on finished woodwork. A nail set should be used to bring the nail head flush with the surface, or just under the surface.

Nails are easy to drive in soft wood but are real "tricky" to handle in hard wood. A thin film of paste wax or soap on the nail will insure better results. Be sure to keep the face of the hammer clean and shiny. For very hard woods it is best to drill a pilot hole.

KINDS AND SIZES

The quality of your nailing job will depend a lot on your judgment when selecting the correct size of hammer and nails.

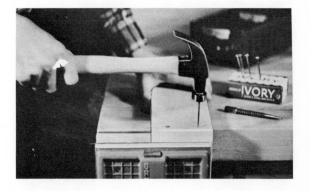

Fig. 8-1. Driving a nail.

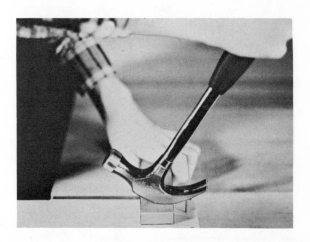

Fig. 8-2. Pulling a nail. Notice wood block placed under hammer to increase leverage and protect the wood surface.

Claw hammers are the standard tools for driving nails. They range in size from 7 oz. to 20 oz. (this is the weight of the head). The most common sizes for the school shop are 10 oz. and 13 oz. Fig. 8-2 shows a 13 oz. hammer being used to draw or pull a nail.

There are many kinds and sizes of nails. Those shown in Fig. 8-3 are standard types that you should be able to readily identify. The common nail has a heavy cross-section and is used for rough carpentry work. The lighter box nail is used for light construction, crating and boxes. The casing nail is the same weight as the box nail, but has a small conical head. As the name implies it is used in finished carpentry work to attach door and window casings and other interior woodworking trim. Finishing nails and brads are quite similar, and have the thinnest cross-section and the smallest head.

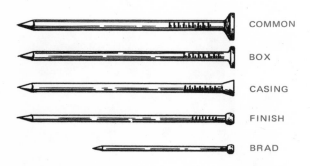

Fig. 8-3. Types of nails.

The nail size is called a "penny," which is abbreviated with the lower case letter d. It indicates the length of the nail. A 2d (2 penny) nail is 1 in. long and increases 1/4 in. for each penny. For example, we could determine the length of a 4d nail by the following: $1 + (2 \times 1/4) = 1\ 1/2$ in. long. An 8d nail would be 2 1/2 in. long. This measurement applies to common, box, casing and finishing nails. Brads are specified by stating their actual length and wire gage number.

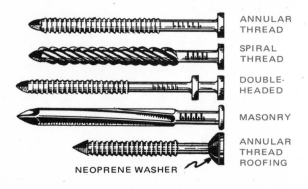

Fig. 8-4. Nails for special purposes.

Fig. 8-4 shows a few of the many specialized nails available today. Each is designed for a special purpose. These nails are made of such materials as iron, steel, copper, bronze, aluminum and stainless steel. Some nails have special coatings of zinc, cement or resin. Coating or threading a nail will increase its holding power three to four times that of a smooth nail.

WOOD SCREWS

Wood screws provide greater holding power than nails and make disassembly of parts easy. However, they require more time to install and are used chiefly in high grade cabinetwork and furniture construction.

The size of wood screws is determined by their length and diameter (gage number). They are classified according to the shape of head (Fig. 8-5), surface finish, and the material from which they are made.

Wood screws are available in lengths from 1/4 to 6 in. and in gage numbers from 0 to 24. The gage number can vary in any given length of screw. For example, you could select a 1 1/2 in. screw with a No. 7 gage, or the same length in a No. 14. The first would be a thin screw, while the second would have a much larger diameter. From one gage number to the next, a wood screw varies by .013 in. (13 thousandths). An average diameter 1 1/2 in. screw would have a gage number of about 10.

Most wood screws are made of mild steel with no special surface finish. They are concealed in the cabinet or furniture structure. Such screws are labeled as F.H.B., which stands for flat head bright. When the screws are to be visible, they should be nickel or chromium plated, or made of brass with an oval or round head.

To completely specify wood screws you should describe them in detail; for example:

10 — 1 1/4 x No. 8 — Round Head — Nickled.

To secure the maximum holding power, select a screw long enough to enter the base piece of wood the entire length of the screw threads. This will be about two thirds of the screw length. Thin stock may not permit this length. You will need to apply good judgment in your selection. The "end grain" of wood does not hold screws well, an extra long screw should be used.

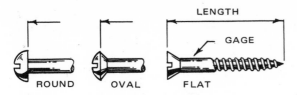

STANDARD SLOTTED SCREWS

PHILLIPS HEAD SCREW

Fig. 8-5. Types of wood screw heads.

Flat and oval-head screws should be countersunk. Use a countersink in a bit brace, and cut just deep enough to fit the underside of the head exactly. Fig. 8-7. Flat-head screws look especially bad if not aligned perfectly with the wood surface.

SCREWDRIVERS

Before you attempt to drive wood screws, be sure the tip of the screwdriver looks like those shown in Fig. 8-8. The tip must be square, the correct width, and fit squarely into the screw slot. To recondition the tip it should be carefully shaped on a grinder, and the ground surfaces honed on an oilstone.

The size of a screwdriver is specified by the length of its blade, measuring from the handle to the tip. They range in size from 1 1/2 to 18 in. The most common sizes for woodworking range from 2 1/2 to 6 in.

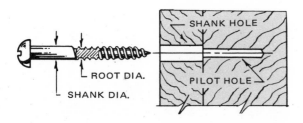

SCREW GAGE	5	6	7	8	9	10	12
SHANK HOLE	1/8	5/32	5/32	3/16	3/16	3/16	7/32
PILOT HOLE	1/16	3/32	3/32	3/32	1/8	1/8	5/32

Fig. 8-6. Approximate drill size to use for some common screw gages.

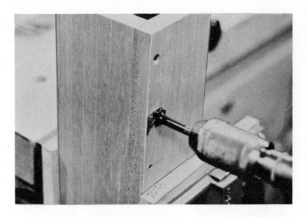

Fig. 8-7. Countersinking for a flat-head screw.

DRILLING HOLES FOR WOOD SCREWS

To fasten wood together with screws, two different size holes should be drilled for each screw. One should be the size of the screw shank, and the second the size or the root diameter of the screw thread, as shown in Fig. 8-6.

Use good judgment in selecting the size of the drill bits. The size of the shank hole should be just large enough so that the screw can be pushed in with the fingers. The size of the pilot hole (sometimes called the anchor hole) for a given screw will vary depending on the hardness of the wood. For example, white pine may not need a pilot hole while with oak or hard maple a pilot hole is essential and must be carefully sized. Pilot holes for very small screws can be made with a brad awl.

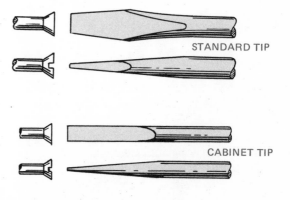

Fig. 8-8. Screwdriver tips.

If you have drilled holes for the screw properly, it's an easy matter to insert the screw in the shank hole and drive it "home" with the screwdriver, Fig. 8-9. Use care that the screwdriver does not slip out of

Fig. 8-9. Driving a 1 3/4 in. No. 9 — F.H.B. screw with a 4 in. screwdriver.

the slot and dent the surface of your work. Using Phillips type screws helps eliminate this problem because the tip cannot easily slip out of the screw slot. A screwdriver bit mounted in a brace or an automatic screwdriver, will save time when you have a large number of screws to set.

As in the case of nails, soap or wax will allow the screw to be driven easier into hard woods. Do not apply too much force as you may twist the screw off. Screws usually break just where the threads start, and are very difficult to remove. Too much force, or a poor screwdriver tip, will damage the slot in the screw head and make your work appear shoddy.

Brass screws are very soft and must be given special care. Sometimes it is worthwhile to first drive a steel screw of the same size (this will cut threads in the pilot hole), then remove and insert the brass screw.

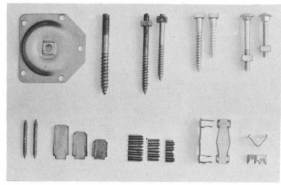

Fig. 8-10. Some special fasteners. Top row — mounting plate, hanger bolts, lag screws, carriage bolts. Bottom row — dowel screws, splines, corrugated fasteners, wood joiners and chevrons.

QUIZ — UNIT 8

1. When driving a nail you must keep your eye on the _____ head.
2. A tool that should be used with the hammer when driving a nail below the surface of the wood is called a _____ .
3. Claw hammers range in size from 7 oz. to _____ oz.
4. The largest size of claw hammer recommended for woodwork in the school shop is a _____ oz.
5. The size of a hammer is based on the weight of its _____ .
6. The type of nail most often used in crating and rough boxes is the _____ .
7. Size of nails is designated by word "penny" and is abbreviated with case letter _____ .
8. The length of a 6 penny nail is _____ in.
9. Brad size should be specified by its length and

_____ number.
10. When nailing a 1 x 4 to a face of a 2 x 4, the largest size of nail you can use and not have it go through the 2 x 4 is a _____ .
11. The size of wood screws is determined by their shank gage and _____ .
12. Wood screw gages vary from 0 to _____ .
13. The next size smaller shank gage of a No. 10 screw would be a No. _____ .
14. The difference in diameter between a No. 12 and No. 14 wood screw would be _____ thousandths of an inch.
15. The wood screw most often used for general construction is labeled with the letters _____ .
16. When setting screws in hard wood it is always best to drill a pilot hole and a _____ hole.
17. The size of a screwdriver is determined by the length of its _____ .

SANDING AND PREPARING FOR FINISH

1. Kinds and grade of abrasive papers.
2. How to use abrasive paper for smoothing wood surface.
3. How to sharpen and use a wood scraper.
4. How to patch defects in wood surfaces.

Sanding is the process of cutting the wood fibers with an abrasive (a hard material that grinds and wears away a softer material). The chief purpose of sanding is to smooth the wood surfaces and prepare them for finishing coats. It is a very important operation because clear finishes tend to magnify defects. Scratches and other imperfections that are almost invisible on the dry wood surface are very noticeable when the finish is applied.

Sanding operations should usually not be started until all edge tool work is complete. There will be times when some shaping of the wood can be accomplished best with abrasive paper (commonly called sandpaper). However, you should never try to make abrasive paper take the place of a plane, chisel or other tool.

KINDS AND GRADES OF ABRASIVE PAPER

Abrasive paper is available in flint, garnet, aluminum oxide and silicon carbide types. Flint, garnet and aluminum oxide are common abrasives used in woodwork. Flint and garnet are natural (mined or quarried) materials, while aluminum oxide and silicon carbide are manufactured. Flint is grayish white in color, inexpensive, and used for rough work. Garnet has a reddish brown color and is a good material for hand sanding. Aluminum oxide is a brown material that appears more tan in color on finer grades of paper. It is hard and tough, and is an excellent abrasive for sanding wood. Aluminum oxide is more expensive than the natural abrasives but will cut faster and wear longer. See Fig. 9-1.

Fig. 9-1. Grades of abrasive paper (enlarged).

50 (1/0)   100 (2/0)   150 (4/0)   220(6/0)   WET-OR-DRY   320—600

The grade of an abrasive depends on the size of the grits (particles). The original method of grading used a number system, referred to as the "aught." A newer method is the mesh system and indicates the number of openings per linear inch of the silk mesh through which the abrasive grits are screened. Listings of abrasive paper grades usually include both the aught number and the mesh number. A wide range of abrasive grades are available. The ones commonly used for woodwork in the school shop are listed below:

	*AUGHT SYSTEM	MESH SYSTEM
Fine	6/0	220
	5/0	180
	4/0	150
Medium	3/0	120
	2/0	100
	1/0	80
Coarse	1/2	60
	1	50

*Gradually being discarded.

These grades apply to garnet and aluminum oxide. Flint paper is usually listed as very fine, fine, medium, coarse and very coarse.

Abrasive papers are packaged in lots of 50 and 100 sheets, called "sleeves." Ten sleeves are called a "unit." The standard sheet size is 9 in. by 11 in. Flint paper is sold in sheets 9 in. by 10 in.

The grade of abrasive paper you select will make considerable difference in the speed and quality of your work. A carefully planed surface can be sanded with a No. 150 paper and be ready for finish. If light tool marks show on the surface, it will probably be best to start with a No. 100, then finish with a No. 150. When changing from a coarse grade to a finer grade, do not move more than two grade numbers. For example, it would take a great deal of sanding with a No. 180 paper to remove the heavy scratches left by a No. 80 paper. Coarse grades of paper are used for such operations as shaping edges or removing gouge marks.

USING ABRASIVE PAPER

As a general rule, each individual piece should be sanded before assembly. Even when all the pieces are

Fig. 9-2. Tearing a strip of abrasive paper along the edge of a steel bench rule.

sanded before assembly, a "touch-up" sanding is needed after assembly.

Sanding should be done in the direction of the wood grain. Abrasive paper will cut faster across the grain. If you have a heavy defect to remove, you may want to resort to this method, but remember you will need to do a great amount of sanding with the grain to remove the "cross grain" scratches.

A full abrasive paper sheet will be too large for your work and will need to be divided into several small pieces. Lay the sheet, grit side down, on a flat surface and tear it along a bench rule or other straight edge, as shown in Fig. 9-2. Coarse grades of paper may need to be folded and creased before tearing.

When sanding flat surfaces, the paper should be mounted or held on a block. The paper will last longer and do better work if the block has a rubber or

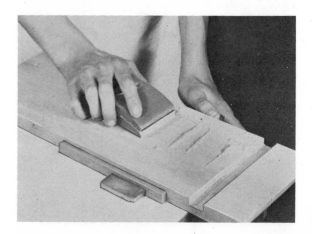

Fig. 9-3. Sanding a wood surface.

felt cushion. The rubber sanding block shown in Fig. 9-3 holds one fourth of a standard sheet.

Before starting to sand a surface, remove pencil marks with a rubber eraser or a scraper. Keep your hands clean during sanding operations and when you handle the work after sanding.

It takes both pressure and motion to make abrasive paper cut. You can apply these best when the wood is held in a vise or clamped to a bench top. Protect sanded surfaces and edges with smooth blocks of scrap wood. Use full strokes and move uniformly over the whole surface. Sand just enough to produce a smooth surface. Excessive sanding on some woods, especially fir, will undercut the soft grain and produce a "wavy" surface. Thin veneers of hardwood plywood must be sanded lightly and carefully.

A sanding block should be used when sanding all edges, chamfers and bevels. Keep the block from rocking so these surfaces will stay flat and not become rounded. Cut out special blocks to fit concave curves and irregular shapes, Fig. 9-4. Some shapes can be sanded with the paper wrapped around a wood file.

Fig. 9-5. Sanding small parts on sanding board.

Fig. 9-6. Sanding a small part. Coarse paper on sanding board "holds" the wood piece while it is being sanded with fine paper on the sanding block.

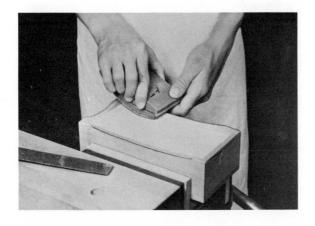

Fig. 9-4. Sanding a curved edge. The abrasive paper has been mounted on the curved side of the rubber sanding block.

SANDING SMALL PIECES

When wood parts are small it is often easier to clamp or hold the abrasive paper against a flat surface and move the wood over it. Fig. 9-5 shows such a procedure using a "sanding board." The board holds a full sheet of paper that is attached with rubber cement. A cleat along the underside is clamped in the vise to hold the board in position. Note Fig. 9-6.

USING A WOOD SCRAPER

If a wood surface has splintered areas because of curly or irregular grain, or ridges left by the plane, it can be smoothed by using a wood scraper. This should be done before the surface is sanded.

The scraper can be either pulled or pushed. It is held at an angle of about 75 deg. The degree will vary, depending on the way the scraper was sharpened. Fig. 9-7 shows a hand scraper in use. A cabinet scraper is the same type of tool, except that the blade is carried in a frame or body.

To sharpen a hand scraper, place it in a vise and draw file the edge square with the sides. Hone this edge and the sides on the oilstone until the corners of the edge are smooth and sharp. With the scraper again

Fig. 9-7. Using a wood scraper.

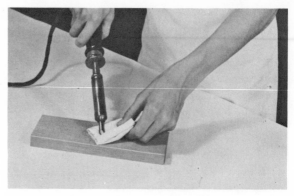

Fig. 9-9. Swelling a dent in wood with a damp cloth and soldering iron.

held in a vise, run a burnisher (hardened steel rod) along the edge. Hold the burnisher at a 90 deg. angle with the sides for the first stroke. Gradually tilt it for the next three or four strokes until it reaches an angle of about 85 deg., Fig. 9-8. Use a drop of oil on the burnisher and press it down firmly. This will form a slight hook or burr on the edge that will cut a fine "silky" shaving.

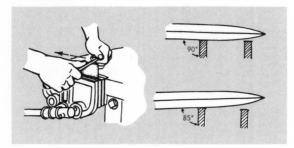

Fig. 9-8. Using a burnisher to turn edge of scraper. (Stanley Tools)

REPAIRING A WOOD SURFACE

To repair a small dent in the wood, place a drop of water in the depression. The water will soak into the wood fibers and swell them back to near their original position. When the dent is large, use a hot soldering iron and damp cloth, Fig. 9-9. Too much steaming or wetting is undesirable, especially when working with interior plywood. Allow the surface to dry thoroughly before sanding.

Checks, cracks and holes can be filled with stick shellac, wood putty, or plastic wood. These materials will not take stain properly and you must select a color that will match the final finish. Stick shellac comes in various colors. It can be melted and applied

with an electrically heated knife. Plastic wood is also available in colors. A natural shade can be tinted with colors in oil as shown in Fig. 9-10. Place a bit of the color in oil on a paper towel and then mix a small portion of plastic wood with it using a putty knife. Keep the plastic wood can covered except when removing some material. If the plastic wood becomes too hard, it can be softened with lacquer thinner.

Fig. 9-10. Coloring plastic wood to patch a hole.

Plastic wood shrinks when it dries, so large patches should be filled above the level of the wood. Sand the patches smooth with the surface of the wood after the plastic has hardened.

THE FINAL TOUCH

When the wood surfaces are sanded smooth and are ready for finish, "soften" all the corners by removing the sharpness, using a pad of fine abrasive paper. With these very slightly rounded corners, there will be less danger of cutting through when rubbing down a coat of finish. Softened corners feel so much better "to the touch" and they also wear better. Be careful that the edge of the abrasive paper does not pick up wood splinters.

Finally, dust the project carefully and go over the surface with a damp sponge, Fig. 9-11. This will swell

Fig. 9-11. Using a damp sponge to moisten surface and raise the wood grain.

tiny wood fibers that have not been completely cut off with the abrasive paper and make them raise above the surface. This is called "raising the grain" and is a very important operation if a water stain is to be used. After the surface is dry, sand very lightly with a fine paper. Again, dust the project carefully and it is ready for the first coat of finish.

QUIZ — UNIT 9

1. The three kinds of abrasives used for sanding wood are flint, garnet and _____ _____ .
2. Abrasives that are mined or quarried are called _____ materials.
3. The grade of an abrasive is determined by the size of the _____ .
4. The next finer grade to a number 1/2 abrasive paper would be a number _____ .
5. It is very important that the sanding motion be in the same direction as the _____ .
6. To sharpen a wood scraper you will need a file, an oilstone and a _____ .
7. Small dents in a wood surface can be removed by applying a few drops of _____ .

Industry Photo. Modern door and panel sizing machine — automatically cuts workpieces to exact size. It takes lots of skill and know-how to set up and maintain high production woodworking machines.   (Jenkins, Div. Kohler-General)

Fig. 10-1. Cabinet for wood finishes.

WOOD FINISHING

1. **Proper sequence for applying finishing coats.**

2. **How to apply stains, fillers and sealers.**

3. **Applying surface coats of lacquer and varnish.**

Wood finishing is an important step in the making of your project. Select and apply the finish carefully and you will add to its beauty as well as protect the surface of the wood.

You should do your share in maintaining the condition of the finishing materials and supplies. Always clean up your materials and return them to their proper place as soon as you have finished with

Fig. 10-2. Cleaning lip of can before replacing the lid.

them. See Figs. 10-1 and 10-2. Use care while working around other students' projects. Don't touch wet surfaces or "spatter" them with a finish you are using.

BRUSHES

There are many sizes, shapes and grades of brushes. The quality of the bristle makes a great difference in how well the brush will hold and spread the finish. A good bristle has a slight taper, is oval in cross-section and has flagged (split) ends as shown in Fig. 10-3. Nylon bristles and Chinese hog bristles have

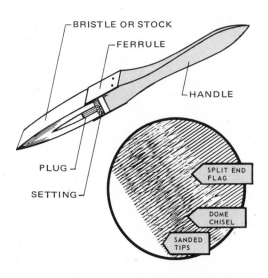

BRISTLE OR STOCK

FERRULE

HANDLE

PLUG

SETTING

SPLIT END FLAG

DOME CHISEL

SANDED TIPS

Fig. 10-3. Parts of a brush. Inset shows the tip of a quality brush.

these characteristics. Nylon bristles wear longer than China bristles, but cannot be used in lacquer and some synthetics.

Brushes that are in use from day to day may be kept suspended in a thinner or in some cases the finish being used. The rubber brush holders shown in the illustrations work well for shellac, lacquer and some synthetic finishes. They are not satisfactory for finishes with an oil base. It is best to thoroughly clean a brush after it has been used in varnish, in paint or enamel.

To clean a brush, first remove as much of the material as possible by pulling it over the edge of the container and then wiping with a rag or paper towel. Fig. 10-4. Wash the brush thoroughly in the correct thinner. Fig. 10-5. Then wipe off as much thinner as possible. Now wash the brush in soap and water, straighten the bristles and wrap in a paper towel. Discard oily rags by taking them to the school incinerator or store them in a covered metal container.

Thinner

Soap and Water

Fig. 10-4. Materials for brush cleaning.

STAINING

Staining is the first step to consider in the finishing schedule. It will emphasize or de-emphasize the grain and will add color to the wood surface. Most stains used on exterior woodwork have a preservative feature. Staining is not essential in obtaining a finished surface. Many woods have the most beauty when finished "natural" using clear finish.

Stains are generally classified in three groups. They are water, oil and spirit (alcohol base). There are two general types of oil stain: penetrating and pigmented. Penetrating stains are brushed on and the excess wiped off. Fig. 10-6. They should dry 24 hours and then be sealed with a thin coat of shellac. Pigment stains are applied in the same manner as penetrating stain. For heavy "toning" or "lightening"

Fig. 10-5. Thinners for wood finishing stored in safety cans.

Fig. 10-6. Applying penetrating oil stain.

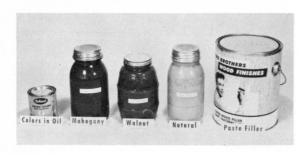

Fig. 10-7. Colors in oil are mixed with natural filler to obtain various shades.

Fig. 10-8. The thin shaving of walnut shows the large pores that require a paste filler.

be filled with a paste filler. Some woodworkers prefer to apply a thin coat of shellac to the wood before the filling operation.

Paste filler contains silex (powdered quartz), linseed oil, turpentine and driers. It can be purchased in a natural shade (very light buff) and in several standard colors. Natural paste filler can be colored by adding colors ground in oil. Fig. 10-7. For a walnut shade use Vandyke brown and burnt umber. For mahogany use Vandyke brown and Venetian red. Thin the filler with turpentine or naphtha to a thin, creamy consistency.

SAMMY SAFETY
SAYS:

"Most finishes are combustible, so keep them away from heat, sparks and open flames. Keep the room well ventilated. Don't leave finishing materials on your hands too long and avoid breathing vapors. Keep containers closed when not in use."

Apply the filler by pouring a small amount onto the wood surface; spread and rub it into the wood pores with the palm of your hand. In a short time (10-20 minutes) the filler will lose its wet appearance and the excess should be wiped off. Use a fairly coarse rag or a piece of burlap, wiping across the grain. Use a rag over a small pointed stick to remove filler from corners. Finish by wiping lightly with the grain. See Fig. 10-9. Inspect your work carefully. The filler should be in the pores and not on the surface of the wood. A stiff brush should be used when applying paste filler to large surfaces.

After the filler has dried overnight, it should be sanded lightly with a No. 180 finishing paper,

effects, they are allowed to dry without wiping. They generally dry in twelve hours, and usually do not require a shellac sealer. Carefully study the manufacturer's directions and instructions on the label. Try out the stain on a scrap of wood before applying it to your project. Use turpentine or a turpentine substitute (mineral spirits) for a thinner.

PASTE FILLER

Walnut, oak, mahogany, and ash are some of the common hard woods that have an open grain (large pores). Fig. 10-8. For most finishes the pores need to

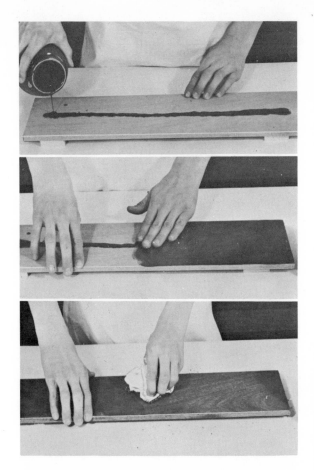

Fig. 10-9. Applying paste filler. Above. Pouring a small amount on the surface. Center. Spreading the filler. Below. Rubbing off across the grain.

working with the wood grain. Paste fillers will vary in the amount of time necessary to completely harden and be ready for additional costs of finish. Check the manufacturer's recommendation.

SEALERS

A sealer may be defined as the first coat of finish applied to close-grained woods such as pine, basswood, cherry and birch, or the first coat after paste filler on open-grained wood. Shellac is commonly used as a sealer. Lacquer based sealer (called sanding sealer) is designed for spraying but is easily brushed on smaller projects. There are many sealers that are especially designed for brush application that have excellent sanding qualities.

When using shellac (4 lb. cut) for a sealer it should be reduced with an equal amount of alcohol. Flow the shellac on with long brush strokes working from

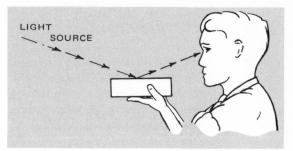

Fig. 10-10. How to inspect a surface.

the center of an area out over the edge. Do not brush back over the work. Allow the shellac to dry for at least two hours, then rub down with steel wool.

Shellac may also be used for the final finish. Apply second and third coats reduced about as much as the sealer coat. Allow overnight drying for all coats and rub each down with steel wool. After the last coat has been rubbed down apply a coat of paste wax.

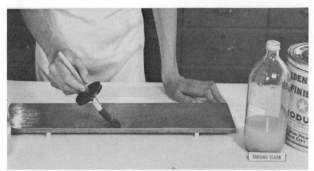

Fig. 10-11. Applying and cutting down sanding sealer.

Sanding sealer, Fig. 10-11, is brushed in the same manner as shellac. It will dry so you can handle your project in about 10 minutes and can usually be sanded with a dry No. 220 paper in 40 to 50 minutes.

SURFACE COATS OF LACQUER AND SYNTHETIC VARNISH

After the wood has been stained, filled and sealed, you are ready to apply the final surface finishes. Many new products are available in the area of synthetic varnishes and brushing lacquers. In using such finishes, always study the manufacturer's recommendations on the label. Some synthetic varnishes require a special thinner.

In applying lacquer and synthetic varnish, as in applying all finishes, the surfaces of your project should be clean. Brush them off carefully and then wipe with a tack-cloth (cloth treated so it will pick up lint and dust). Commercially prepared tack-cloths are available at reasonable cost.

Thin the finish if necessary, so it will flow easily. Dip the brush in the material so about one-third of the bristle length is immersed. Rub the brush against the inside edge of the container to remove the excess material. In applying finishing material to your project, move the brush over the surface with just enough pressure to cause the bristles to bend a little. Use fairly long strokes in the same direction as the grain of the wood. Work rather quickly, completing one section at a time. See Figs. 10-12 to 10-14 inclusive. Do not go back over a surface once it has been coated. Work from the center of a surface out over the edges. Keep the surface being coated between you and major light source so that you will have a good view of the work, Fig. 10-10.

Usually it is best to coat "hard-to-get-at" surfaces first. Brush edges and ends before the faces; bottoms before the tops. On some jobs you may find it best to coat the bottom surfaces, allow them to dry, then turn the project over and do the sides and top. You can make a tripod on which to rest the work by driving nails all the way through a thin piece of wood. Some pieces may be coated all over, then hung by a string or wire to dry.

On most projects, you should apply at least two coats of varnish or lacquer. The first coat should be cut down dry with 3/0 steel wool or No. 220 finishing paper. Clean the surface carefully and apply a second coat.

Rubber brush holders and mason jars save a lot of brush cleaning when these finishes are used a great deal. They are not "foolproof," however, and will

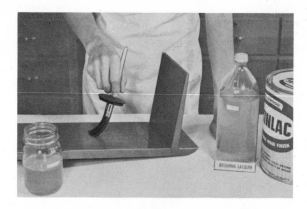

Fig. 10-12. Brushing a coat of lacquer.

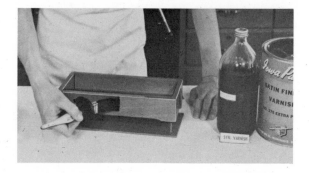

Fig. 10-13. Applying synthetic varnish.

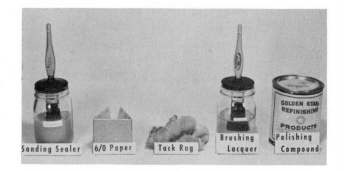

Fig. 10-14. Materials for lacquer finish.

require complete cleaning from time to time. Each time you finish using the material, you should wipe off the jar and bring the level of the finish to a mid-point on the bristles of the brush.

PENETRATING SEALER

A penetrating sealer is also referred to as a "rub-on" finish. It will produce a good finish and is

Fig. 10-15. Materials for applying a penetrating finish.

Fig. 10-16. Rubbing on penetrating finish.

Fig. 10-17. Cutting finish with steel wool.

Fig. 10-18. Applying enamel.

very easy to apply. There are a number of brands available such as Dura-seal, Sealacell and Minwax.

For a natural finish on close-grained wood, pour a small amount of the finish on the surface and spread it with a soft cloth. Allow it to dry 24 hours, then rub it down with 3/0 steel wool. Second and third coats applied in the same manner but somewhat more sparingly, will give a smooth satin finish.

A penetrating seal can be applied over stain and/or filler. Use the same procedure as just described. Some woodworkers prefer to apply a coat of penetrating sealer before using paste filler.

After the last coat of sealer is rubbed down a coat of paste wax may be applied. See Figs. 10-15 to 10-17 inclusive.

PAINT AND ENAMEL

If you build your project of wood that does not have an attractive grain pattern, you may want to finish it with paint or enamel. Fig. 10-18. Seal any knots or sap streaks with shellac. Brush on a coat of enamel undercoater. After it is dry, sand it lightly, then apply a coat of enamel. If it is necessary to apply a second coat of enamel, the first coat should be cut lightly with fine abrasive paper. Use turpentine or mineral spirits for thinning these materials and also for cleaning the brush.

Latex emulsion paints make a satisfactory finish for wall shelves, picture frames, and other projects that are not subjected to hard usage. These paints have many advantages. They are easy to apply and dry quickly. They require no undercoat and water is used for thinner. They are available in a wide range of colors. Brushes should be cleaned in soap and water immediately after use.

SANDING AND RUBBING FINISHED SURFACES

Cutting down finished surfaces with abrasive paper, steel wool, or a powdered abrasive is an important part of producing a good finish. If brush marks, dust specks and other imperfections are not removed, they will continue as a part of the finish and even become more noticeable after the next coat is applied.

First coats should be rubbed with dry finishing paper or steel wool. At this stage the finish is quite thin and water or other lubricants could easily get under the surface. Use a small piece of abrasive paper and fold it twice into equal sections. This makes a good "pad" with the grain side of one flap interlocking with the paper side of the other flap. Always clean the surface carefully after rubbing, especially when steel wool is used.

When cutting the second coat with abrasives (and any succeeding coats) you will find that a wet-or-dry silicon carbide paper used with water works very well. A 400 or 500 grade paper will remove imperfections and leave a dull sheen to the surface. A brighter sheen can be obtained by rubbing with pumice stone and oil, or rottenstone and oil. A commercially prepared rubbing compound is recommended for polishing the final coat of lacquer. Finishes should always be rubbed in the direction of the wood grain.

Finishes are available that dry to a soft, rubbed-effect lustre and do not require a final rubbing or polishing.

Fig. 10-19. Skilled workers produce special effects on high quality furniture. (Thomasville Furniture Industries, Inc.)

FINISHING SCHEDULES

It is good practice to develop a finishing schedule, and include it in your plan of procedure. This will make it easy for your teacher to check your ideas and make suggestions.

Listed below is a sample of a schedule you might prepare for a lacquer finish on walnut, mahogany or other open-grained wood:

1. Apply a pigment oil stain. Dry at least 12 hours.

Skilled workers spraying final coat of lacquer in a modern furniture plant. Units rest on pallets which are carried on a conveyor line. (Mersman Bros. Corp.)

2. Fill with a paste filler, colored to match the stain. Dry overnight.
3. Sand very lightly with No. 180 paper and clean the surface.
4. Brush one coat of sanding sealer. Dry 1 hour.
5. Rub down sanding sealer with No. 220 paper, brush off surface and wipe with a tack rag.
6. Apply clear brushing lacquer. Dry 4 hours.
7. Rub with No. 220 paper or 3/0 steel wool.
8. Apply second coat of clear brushing lacquer. Dry overnight.
9. Rub with polishing compound.

FINISHING IN INDUSTRY

Brush application of finishes is too slow and expensive for modern production lines. Spray finishing with fast drying lacquers and synthetics helps to make it possible to purchase quality products at moderate prices.

Small wooden objects such as golf tees, knobs, buttons, fishing plugs, beads and blocks are finished by "tumbling." In this process the parts are placed in a large drum or barrel with especially prepared enamels and lacquers. The drum is turned at a speed of about 25 rpm, causing the small parts to roll and tumble over each other as they dry. This results in a smooth, satiny finish that is impossible to duplicate by any other method.

Other production methods of finishing include: roller coating, dipping and flow coating. Some use is made of these methods to finish woodwork but they are more adaptable to metal parts.

A study of the whole area of finishing could easily become a course in itself. Entire books are devoted to the subject. The chemical industry continues to provide many new and improved types of synthetic finishes to extend this study. The wood finisher and painter of today faces a great challenge as he keeps abreast of many new techniques and materials.

QUIZ — UNIT 10

1. One of the important qualities of a true brush bristle is that it has _____ ends.
2. After paste wood filler has set-up for 10 or 20 minutes it should be wiped off_____ the grain of the wood.
3. Mahogany is one of the common hard woods that has an _____ grain.
4. Paste wood filler should be thinned with naphtha or _____ .
5. A rag that has been especially treated to pick up lint and dust particles is called a_____ .
6. If the shellac is too heavy for easy brushing it should be thinned with _____ .
7. Sanding sealer should be cut down with a dry paper of about _____ grade.
8. A penetrating sealer should dry _____ hours before being cut down and recoated.
9. Undercoater should dry thoroughly and then be _____ before a coat of enamel is applied.
10. Latex emulsion paints should be thinned with _____ .
11. Water or oil should not be used in rubbing down a finish until the _____ surface coat has been applied.
12. Mineral spirits is a petroleum product used as a substitute for _____ .
13. The liquid part of a paint is called the _____ .

DRILL PRESS, JIG SAW, BAND SAW

1. **How to use the drill press.**
2. **How to install blades in a jig saw.**
3. **How to make internal cuts on a jig saw.**
4. **Operating a band saw efficiently and safely.**

THE DRILL PRESS

The size of a drill press is indicated in terms of diameter of the largest circular piece which may be drilled through the center while on the table of the drill press. The 15 in. drill press shown in Fig. 11-1 will drill a hole in the center of a round piece 15 in. in diameter. A drill press is used chiefly for drilling holes, but with special attachments it may be used for drum sanding, mortising, shaping and routing.

In preparing to use a drill press, lay out and mark the center of the hole in the same manner as when working with hand tools. Insert a bit into the key chuck as far as it will go, and turn the chuck by hand until the jaws are snug on the drill. Use the chuck key to tighten the chuck. Always remove the chuck key from the chuck immediately after use.

Fig. 11-2. Boring a 3/4 in. hole.

Adjust the height of the table and the depth stop so that the vertical travel of the drill will be correct for your work. The center hole of the table should be directly under the bit.

Use the slowest speed for holes that are over 1/4 in. in diameter. Smaller diameters can be drilled

Fig. 11-1. Photo of a drill press.   (Rockwell Mfg. Co.)

VARIABLE SPEED CONTROL

SAFETY SWITCH

QUILL LOCK

KEY CHUCK

TILTING TABLE

INDEX PIN

BASE

BELT GUARD

DEPTH STOP

HEAD SUPPORT SAFETY COLLAR

FEED LEVER

TABLE LOCKING CLAMP

COLUMN

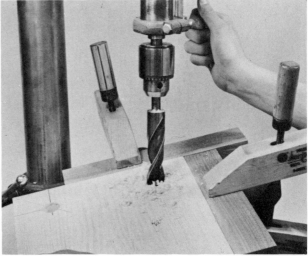

Fig. 11-3. Left. Special setup for drilling hole in small part. Drill the hole half way through, reverse the piece and finish from the other end. Fig. 11-4. Right. Drilling holes at an angle by tilting the table. Strips clamped on the table make it easy to locate a hole in each corner of the stock.

safely at higher speeds. Check with your instructor before changing the speed of the drill press.

Hold the work firmly in the correct position on the table. Turn on the drill and feed the bit into the work with the feed lever. Use just enough pressure so the drill cuts easily. For large holes in small pieces of wood you should mount the work in a drill press vise, or clamp it to the table.

If the hole is to go all the way through the stock, use a piece of scrap stock under your work. See Fig. 11-2. When drilling deep holes with a small bit, withdraw bit several times to remove cuttings.

Always stop the machine before making any adjustments. Special setups are shown in Figs. 11-3 and 11-4.

THE JIG SAW

The size of a jig saw (sometimes called a scroll saw) is determined by the distance from the blade to the over arm. You can cut to the center of a 48 in. circle on a 24 in. saw. The jig saw is an excellent tool to use for cutting sharp curves and various shapes in thin wood, Fig. 11-5.

CUTTING ON THE JIG SAW

Loosen the guide post and position the guide assembly so that the hold-down springs rest firmly on the top of the work. Start the saw and feed the work

forward into the blade. You will get the smoothest cut if you feed the work slowly. Keep the blade cutting just on the outside or "waste side" of the line. Give the blade plenty of time to cut its way clear as you go around corners.

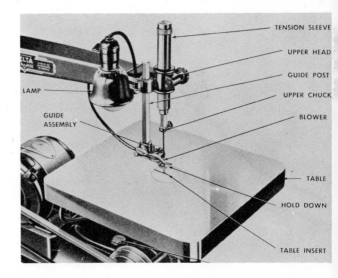

Fig. 11-5. Parts of a jig saw.

Before cutting complicated designs, you should work out the "route" you will follow. This will often eliminate the need to back out of long cuts, or make sharper turns than the blade permits. Drilling small holes in the waste stock at corners will often make the cutting easier. See Figs. 11-6, 11-7 and 11-8.

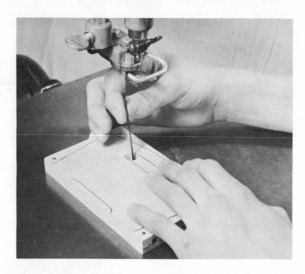

Fig. 11-6. Threading jig saw blade for internal cutting. Detach blade from upper chuck and roll machine by hand until the blade is at its lower point before threading the blade through the work.

Jig saw blades vary in length, width and thickness. They also vary in the number of teeth per inch and the shape of the teeth. Study a manufacturer's catalog for suggestions on blade selection for special jobs. Most of your work can probably be done with a blade of the following size: .020 in. thick x .110 in. wide — 15 teeth per inch.

INSTALLING BLADE IN JIG SAW

To install a blade in a jig saw remove the table insert and turn the saw by hand until the lower chuck is at its highest point. Loosen the thumbscrew of the lower chuck and see that the jaws are clean. Insert the blade about 1/2 in. with the teeth pointing downward. Hold the blade straight up-and-down and tighten the thumbscrew.

GENERAL SAFETY RULES FOR OPERATING WOODWORKING MACHINES

SAMMY SAFETY
Says:

"As a beginning student you will be expected to do most of your work with hand tools. There will be times, however, when a basic machine operation will save time and be appropriate for your work.

Whether or not you are permitted to use the machines will depend on your own maturity and ability and the policies established by your instructor.

Before operating any power tool or machine you must become thoroughly familiar with the way it operates and how it is used. As you learn to use a machine the correct way, you will also be learning to use it the safe way.

You should know and understand the following general safety rules for power machine operation. In addition, you should also study and follow safety rules that apply to specific machines.

1. Always be sure you have the instructor's approval to operate a machine. He knows you and the machine and can best make the decision as to whether you have "what it takes" to operate it safely.

2. Wear snug-fitting clothing. Roll up your sleeves, tuck in your tie, wear a shop apron and tie it snugly.

3. You must be wide awake and alert. Never operate a machine when you are over tired or ill.

4. Think through the operation before performing it. Know what you are going to do, and what the machine will do.

5. Make all the necessary adjustments before turning on the machine. Some adjustments on certain machines will require the instructor's approval.

6. Never remove or adjust a safety guard without the instructor's permission.

7. Keep the machine tables and working surfaces clear of tools, stock, and project materials. Also keep the floor free of scraps and excessive litter.

8. Allow the machine to reach its full operating speed before starting to feed the work.

9. Feed the work carefully and only as fast as the machine will cut it easily.

10. If a machine is dull, out of adjustment, or in some way not working properly, shut off the power immediately and inform the instructor.

11. You are the one to control the operation. Start and stop the machine yourself. If someone is helping you, be sure they understand this and know what they are expected to do and how do do it.

12. Do not allow your attention to be distracted while operating a machine. Also, be certain that you do not distract the attention of other machine operators.

13. Stay clear of machines being operated by other students. See that other students are "out of the way" when you are operating a machine.

14. When you have completed an operation on a machine, shut off the power and wait until it stops before leaving the machine or setting up another cut. Never leave a machine running and unattended.

15. Machines should not be used for trivial operations, especially on small pieces of stock. Do not play with machines.

16. Do not "crowd around" or wait in line to use a machine. Ask the present operator to inform you at your work station when he has finished. Common standards of courtesy may slow you down a little but they will make the shop a more pleasant and safer place to work."

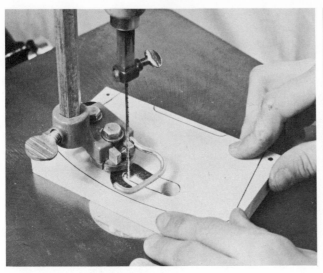
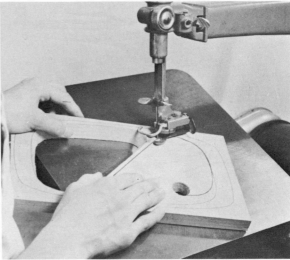

Fig. 11-7. Left. Making an internal cut. Two pieces are being cut. Notice the nails in the waste stock. Fig. 11-8. Right. Making an angle cut. Table and hold down have been tilted 20 degrees.

Loosen the thumbscrew on the upper chuck. Pull the chuck down over the blade and tighten the thumbscrew. Do not use pliers or wrenches to tighten thumbscrews. Position the tension sleeve so it is about 3/4 in. above the upper chuck. Roll the saw over a few turns by hand to see if the blade is clear and runs up and down in a straight line.

Adjust the guide assembly so the blade runs freely on its sides, and the blade support roller just touches the back of the blade. Replace the table insert.

THE BAND SAW

The size of a band saw, Fig. 11-9, is derived from the diameter of its wheels. These wheels are fitted with rubber tires that provide traction for the blade and cushion the teeth. The upper wheel is adjustable up and down to provide tension on the blade. It can also be tilted in or out so that the blade will run in the center of the wheel. This is called "tracking the blade."

The blade guide assemblies are important parts of the band saw. One is located above and the other below the table. The guide above the table, Fig. 11-10, can be moved up and down to adjust for various thicknesses of stock. When perfectly adjusted, the blade guides do not contact the blade except when a piece of wood is being cut. It's a "tricky" job to adjust and line up the band saw blade and guides.

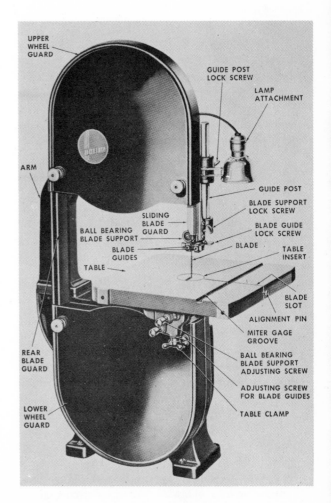

Fig. 11-9. Parts of a band saw.

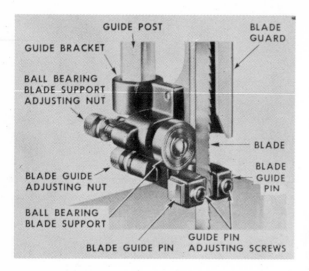

Fig. 11-10. Parts of band saw upper guide assembly.

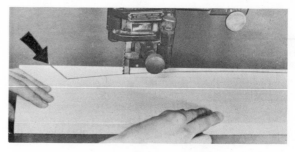

Fig. 11-11. Cutting procedure on the band saw. Arrow points to the cut that was made first.

Fig. 11-12. Relief cuts are made before cutting sharp curves. Notice that the blade is cutting about 1/16 in. on the waste side of the line.

Always check with your instructor before making any of these adjustments.

The band saw is designed to cut curves and irregular shapes in thicker and heavier stock than can be cut on a jig saw. It has a wider blade (usually about 3/8 in.) which cuts faster but not as smooth. The minimum turning radius varies with the blade width and set of the teeth. A 3/8 in. blade should not be used to cut a radius smaller than 1 1/4 inches.

The band saw is often used to rough out stock before planing and jointing.

Some band saws are equipped with rip fences and miter gages, so they may be used in about the same manner as a circular saw.

CUTTING ON THE BAND SAW

Before turning on the machine, adjust the upper guide assembly so that it is about 1/4 in. above the top surface of your stock. Turn on the machine. Use your right hand to push the stock into the saw blade, and your left hand to guide the stock. Because of the rougher cut of the band saw you should stay at least 1/16 in. away from the line.

Make short cuts before long ones as shown in Fig. 11-11. This will prevent the need to back out of a long cut. When possible, cut through waste stock rather than back out. Make several relief cuts before cutting a sharp curve as shown in Fig. 11-12. If the

layout is complicated it should first be "roughed out," cutting only those curves that can be handled easily. After completing these cuts, go back over the work and cut the sharper curves and smaller detail.

BAND SAW SAFETY RULES

SAMMY SAFETY
SAYS:

"1. Adjust the upper guide assembly so it is 1/4 in. above the work before turning on the saw.
2. Allow the saw to reach full speed before starting to feed the work into it.
3. The stock must be held flat on the table.
4. Feed the saw only as fast as the teeth will remove the wood easily.

Fig. 11-13. Left. Using a push stick to maintain a 3 in. margin of safety. Fig. 11-14. Right. Electric saber saw. The tool is well suited for cutting curves and openings in large sheets of plywood.

5. Maintain a 3 in. margin of safety, Fig. 11-13. (This means that the hands should always be at least three inches away from the blade when the saw is running.)

6. Plan saw cuts to avoid "backing out" of curves, wherever possible.

7. Make turns carefully and do not turn radii small enough to cause twisting of blade.

8. If you hear a clicking noise, turn off the machine at once. This indicates a crack in the blade.

9. Round stock should not be cut unless mounted securely in a jig or hand screw.

10. Keep saw evenly set and sharp."

QUIZ — UNIT 11

1. A 14 in. drill press will have a measurement of _____ in. from the center of the chuck to the column.

2. The bit is mounted in the _____ of a drill press.

3. The movable sleeve that carries the spindle of the drill press is called a _____ .

4. Holes can be bored at an angle on the drill press by tilting the _____ .

5. The size of a jig saw is determined by the distance from the blade to the _____ .

6. The blade of a jig saw should be installed with the teeth pointing _____ .

7. A screw that is designed for tightening with the thumb and fingers is called a _____ .

8. The blade support roller on the jig saw should just touch the _____ of the blade.

9. A jig saw blade for general purpose work will have about _____ teeth per inch.

10. The size of a band saw is determined by the size of its _____ .

11. Tilting the top wheel of the band saw in or out to make the blade run in the center of the tire is called _____ the blade.

12. The upper blade guide assembly should be positioned about _____ in. above the top surface of the work.

13. When operating the band saw you should maintain a _____ in. margin of safety.

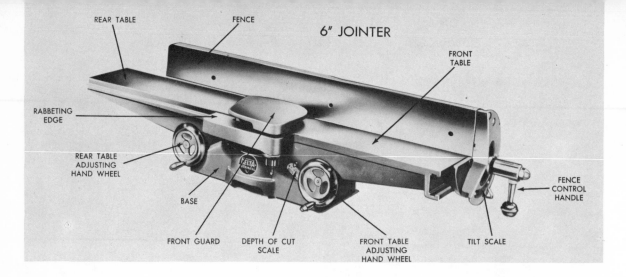

6" JOINTER

REAR TABLE

FENCE

FRONT TABLE

RABBETING EDGE

REAR TABLE ADJUSTING HAND WHEEL

BASE

FRONT GUARD

DEPTH OF CUT SCALE

FRONT TABLE ADJUSTING HAND WHEEL

TILT SCALE

FENCE CONTROL HANDLE

Fig. 12-1. The parts of a jointer.
(Rockwell Mfg. Co.)

JOINTER AND CIRCULAR SAW

1. The wood jointer and its parts.
2. How to perform basic operations on the jointer.
3. How to do ripping and crosscutting on the circular saw.
4. Safety rules for operating the jointer and circular saw.

THE JOINTER AND ITS PARTS

The wood jointer is a power driven machine used to plane or finish edges and surfaces of lumber. A jointer can also be used to cut chamfers, bevels, tapers and rabbets.

Principal parts of a jointer are shown in Fig. 12-1. The cutter head (not shown in the photo) holds three knives and revolves at a speed of about 4500 rpm. The size of the jointer is determined by the length of these knives. This also determines the maximum width of stock the jointer will smooth at one time.

ADJUSTING THE JOINTER

The three main parts that can be adjusted are the front table, the rear table and the fence. The rear table must be level with the knife edges at their highest point of rotation. This is a critical adjustment. Be sure to check with your instructor before making any changes in the setting.

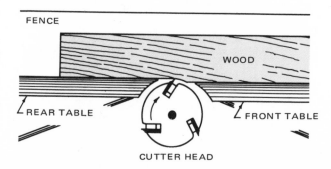

FENCE

WOOD

REAR TABLE

FRONT TABLE

CUTTER HEAD

Fig. 12-2. How a jointer works. Note the direction of the wood grain.

The fence guides the stock over the table and knives. When jointing an edge or squaring stock, it should be perpendicular to the table surface. The fence can be tilted to other angles when cutting chamfers or bevels.

To make a cut on the jointer the front table is set below the level of the knives and rear table. Most jointers have a scale that indicates this distance, which is referred to as the "depth of cut."

JOINTING AN EDGE

Examine your stock and determine the direction of the grain. Turn it to feed into the machine as shown in Fig. 12-2. Be certain that the fence is tight and the guard is in position. Set the depth of cut at about 1/16 in. and start the machine.

Place the stock on the table, hold it against the fence and start the cut as shown in Fig. 12-3. When a foot or more of the stock has passed over the knives, "step" the left hand across the knives and press the stock against the fence and rear table as you continue to move it forward.

JOINTER SAFETY RULES

(These are in addition to general safety rules for operating power-driven machines.)

SAMMY SAFETY
SAYS:

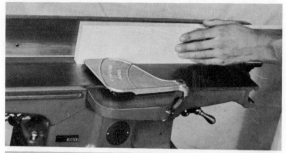

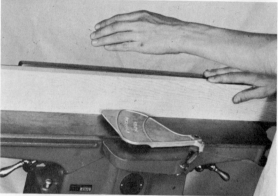

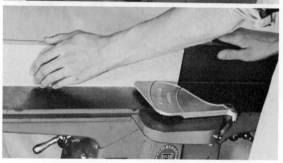

Fig. 12-3. Jointing an edge. Above. Starting the cut. Center. Stepping left hand over the knives. Below. Finishing the cut.

"1. Be sure you have the instructor's approval to operate the machine.

2. Before turning on the machine, make adjustments for depth of cut and position of fence. Do not adjust the rear table or remove the guard.

3. The maximum cut for jointing an edge is 1/8 in. and for a flat surface, 1/16 in.

4. Stock must be at least 12 in. long. Stock to be surfaced must be at least 3/8 in. thick, Fig. 12-6.

5. Feed the work so the knives will cut "with the grain." Use only new stock that is free of knots, splits and checks.

6. Keep your hands away from the cutter head even though the guard is in position. Maintain a 4 in. margin of safety.

7. Use a push block when planing a flat surface.

8. Do not plane end grain.

9. The jointer knives must be sharp. Dull knives will vibrate the stock and may cause a kickback."

For long pieces continue to feed the stock with both hands, first moving one hand back to a new position and then the other. You can finish the cut with the left hand as shown in Fig. 12-3, or you may step the right hand across the knives and finish the cut with both hands.

By following the above procedure, your hands do not pass directly over the knives. Neither is it necessary for them to come closer than four inches to the knives, thus maintaining the margin of safety recommended for the jointer. See Fig. 12-4.

PLANING A SURFACE

Turn your stock so you will be feeding the grain of the wood in the right direction. If there is some warp

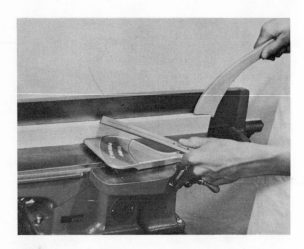

Fig. 12-4. Using push sticks to joint a small strip. Push stick in the right hand is picked up when the end of the stock comes onto the front table.

in the board, turn the concave (dished in) surface downward so that the stock will not rock on the table. Set the depth of cut at about 1/32 in., check the fence and guard, and turn on the machine.

Place the stock on the front table and move it into the knives. The left hand should be kept well back of the knives and then "stepped" over them to hold the stock down on the rear table. Finish the cut by placing a "push block" on the end of the board as shown in Fig. 12-5.

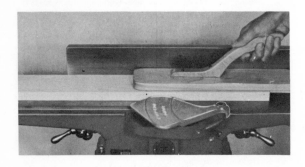

Fig. 12-5. Planing a surface with the aid of a push block.

Thin, narrow strips can be surfaced with considerable safety by using the setup shown in Fig. 12-6. Here a feather board is clamped to the fence so that it applies firm pressure to the stock as it passes over the knives. Feed the stock in about half way, then move around to the rear table and pull it through. The stock should be at least 2 ft. long.

SIZE LIMITATIONS

Small pieces of stock cannot be machined safely on a jointer. For most machines the minimum length is 12 in. The minimum thickness that should be surfaced is 3/8 in. Even with these sizes and larger pieces you will need to use push sticks and push blocks to maintain the 4 in. margin of safety.

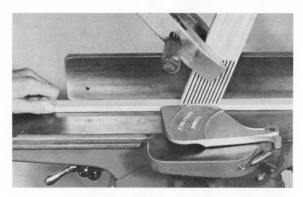

Fig. 12-6. Surfacing a thin strip. Feather board insures safe and accurate work.

Plan your work so that you will machine your stock while it is in large pieces. After it is cut into small pieces you should use hand tools.

THE CIRCULAR SAW

The size of a circular saw is determined by the largest blade it will take. A saw that takes a 10 in. diameter blade, for example, would be called a 10 in. circular saw.

There are three principal types of blades: Rip, Crosscut and Combination. A combination blade will do both ripping and crosscutting, and is the type most often used in the school shop.

Parts of a circular saw are shown in Fig. 12-7.

Before stock is cut on the circular saw, it must be planed or surfaced so it will lay flat on the table. At least one edge must be planed or jointed straight and true.

RIPPING STOCK TO WIDTH

Raise the saw blade until it projects above the table a distance equal to the thickness of the stock

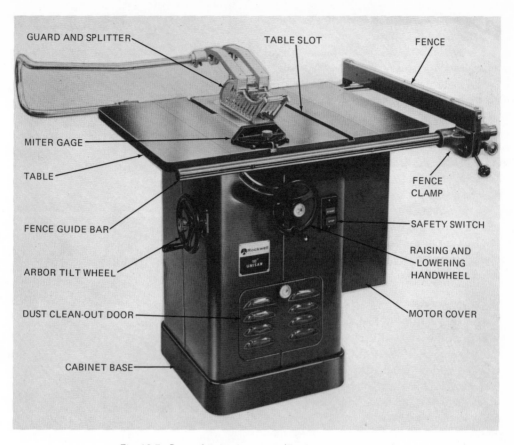

Fig. 12-7. Parts of a circular saw. (Rockwell International)

plus 1/4 in. Unlock the fence and move it along the guide bar to the required width. For a very accurate setting check the measurement between the fence and the point of a tooth on the blade that is set (bent) toward the fence. Lock the fence in position, place the guard over the blade, and start the machine.

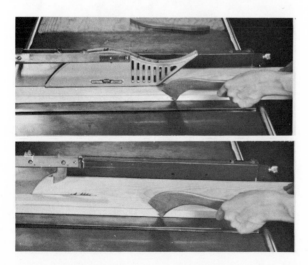

Fig. 12-8. Ripping stock to width. Guard has been raised in the lower picture to show splitter and blade height.

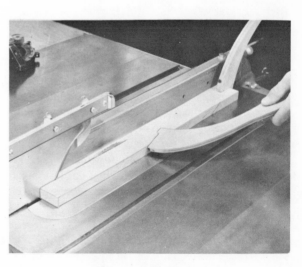

Fig. 12-9. Using push sticks to rip narrow strip. Guard cannot be used.

Place the stock flat on the table with the straight edge against the fence and move it into the blade. Continue a steady feed through the entire cut. Keep your hands at least 4 in. away from the blade even though it is covered by a guard. On narrow stock, use push sticks to maintain this margin of safety, Fig. 12-9. When the saw is operating, stand slightly to one side of the cutting line.

CUTTING STOCK TO LENGTH

Square a line across the stock where the cut is to be made. Set the height of the saw the same as for ripping (1/4 in. above the work). Move the fence to one side and well out of the way. Place the miter gage in the table slot and set it at a right angle (90 deg. mark on the protractor scale).

Hold the straightedge of the stock against the miter gage with your left hand, Fig. 12-10. Align the cutting marks with the saw blade so that the saw kerf will be on the waste side of the line. Lower the guard over the saw and turn on the motor. Grasp the knob of the miter gage in the right hand and move the stock through the cut as shown in Fig. 12-12. Turn off the saw immediately and wait for the blade to stop before leaving the machine or setting up for the next cut.

Maintain the same margin of safety (4 in.) as for ripping. The clamp attachment for the miter gage, shown in Fig. 12-11, increases the accuracy and safety of crosscutting operations.

RESAWING

Resawing is a ripping operation where the thickness of a board is reduced or the board is made into two thinner pieces. If the width of the board does not exceed the maximum height that the blade can be raised, the operation can be completed in one cut. For wider boards set the saw to cut a little above the center line and make two cuts. Keep the same face of the stock against the fence for both cuts. Fig. 12-12 shows a resawing setup with the first cut just being started. A feather board increases the accuracy and safety of resawing operations.

A feather board can be made by ripping a series of saw kerfs about 1/4 in. apart in the end of a board and then trimming it off at about a 30 deg. angle. The strips that are formed serve as a series of "springs" that apply a smooth, even pressure.

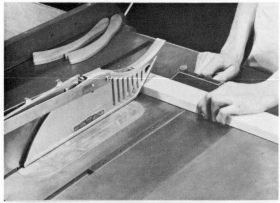

Fig. 12-10. Cutting stock to length. Guard has been removed in lower picture to show height of saw.

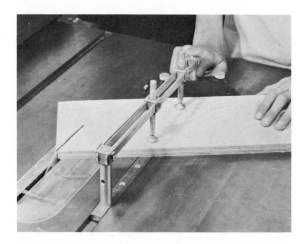

Fig. 12-11. Using a clamp attachment to cut an angle. The guard can be used for this operation.

Beginning students should perform their first resawing operations by setting the saw slightly below the center of the work, leaving about 1/4 in. to hold the two pieces together after the second cut. The pieces can then be cut apart with a handsaw.

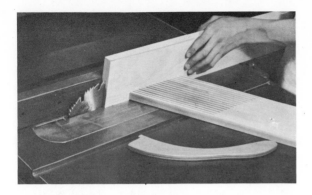

Fig. 12-12. Resawing with the aid of a feather board. Notice that the feather board is positioned just ahead of the saw. The clamp holding the feather board does not show in the picture.

CUT RABBETS WITH THE GRAIN

A rabbet is made with two ripping cuts. Lay out the rabbet on the end of the stock, then measure carefully the height of the saw and the fence setting for each cut. Fig. 12-13 shows the second cut of a rabbet being made. If the order of making the cuts is reversed there is a possibility of a kickback of the waste strip since it would be trapped under the work between the balde and the fence.

Fig. 12-13. Cutting a rabbet. This shows the second cut being made.

THE DADO HEAD

A dado head is designed to cut dados and grooves. It consists of two outside blades with chippers in between. The thickness of the dado can be varied by the number and thickness of the chippers used. Fig. 12-14 shows a dado head being set up. The chippers have wide cutting edges and must be positioned in the

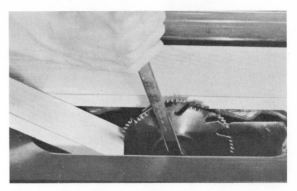

Fig. 12-14. Tightening the dado head.

gullets of the outside blades. A special table insert must be used with a dado head. Always have your instructor check the dado head setup before turning on the power.

Dados and grooves can also be made with the regular saw blade by making a series of cuts and then finishing with a chisel or router plane.

Fig. 12-15. Cutting a groove with the dado head.

CIRCULAR SAW SAFETY

SAMMY SAFETY SAYS:

"1. Be sure the blade is sharp and the right one for your work.

2. Be sure the saw is equipped with a guard and a splitter, and use them.

3. Set the blade so it extends only about 1/4 in. above the stock to be cut.

4. Stand to one side of the operating blade and do not reach across it.

5. Maintain a 4 in. margin of safety. (Do not let your hands come closer than 4 in. to the operating blade even though the guard is in position.)

6. Stock must be surfaced and at least one edge jointed before being cut on the saw.

7. The position of the stock must be controlled either by the fence or the miter gage. Never cut stock free hand.

8. Use only new stock that is free of knots, splits and warp.

9. Stop the saw before adjusting the fence or blade.

10. Do not let small scrap cuttings accumulate around the saw blade. Use a push stick to move them away.''

QUIZ — UNIT 12

1. The size of a jointer is determined by the length of the _____ .

2. The depth of cut of a jointer is controlled by the setting of the _____ _____ .

3. When jointing an edge the fence of the jointer should set at a _____ deg. angle with the table.

4. The minimum length of stock that should be cut on the jointer is _____ inches.

5. When starting to plane an edge joint, the stock should be placed on the front table of the jointer and pressed firmly against the _____ .

6. When surfacing a board that is warped, the concave surface should be turned _____ .

7. Two general types of circular saws are the tilting arbor and the tilting _____ .

8. The height of the saw blade should be about _____ in. above the stock being cut.

9. To square the end of a piece of stock the miter gage should be set on the _____ deg. mark of the protractor scale.

10. When a 3/4 in. board is cut in such a way as to produce two boards 5/16 of an inch thick the operation is called _____ .

Using an auxiliary table on the circular saw. Parts are being cut to exact length. Table unit is guided by strips that slide in the saw table slots. Guard over blade has an acrylic plastic top so cutting action can be observed. (See arrow.)

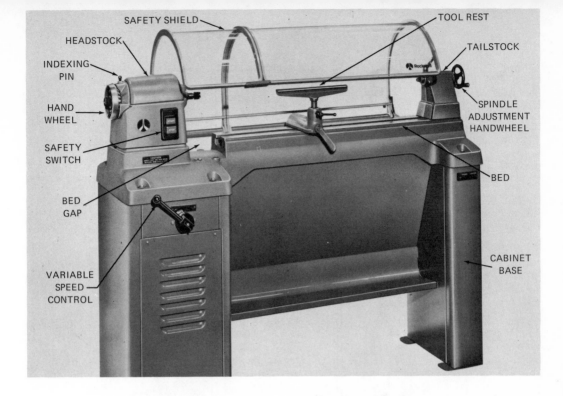

Fig. 13-1. Parts of the wood turning lathe. (Rockwell International)

WOOD LATHE

1. **The wood lathe and its parts.**

2. **How to mount work for spindle turning.**

3. **How to turn small bowls and trays.**

A wood lathe is a power tool on which the wood is mounted and rotated against a cutting edge.

The size of a wood lathe is determined by the largest diameter stock that can be turned on the lathe. The basic parts of a wood lathe are called out in Fig. 13-1.

When stock is mounted between lathe centers and turned, the operation is called spindle turning. This type of turning is used to produce table and chair legs, lamp stems, ball bats and other long round objects. Faceplate turning, where the stock being turned is mounted on the faceplate, is the other general type, and is used for bowls, wheels and other disc-shaped objects.

MOUNTING STOCK FOR SPINDLE TURNING

The stock should be approximately square. Allow an extra inch of length so that the piece can be trimmed after the turning is complete.

Locate the center of each end by drawing diagonal lines across the corners. On the end that will take the spur or drive center, drill a small hole and make saw cuts, Fig. 13-2. Plane off the corners of stock that is more than 2 in. square. Place the stock on the lathe bed and drive the spur center into the work.

Place the spur center, with the wood attached, into the spindle of the head stock and slide the tail

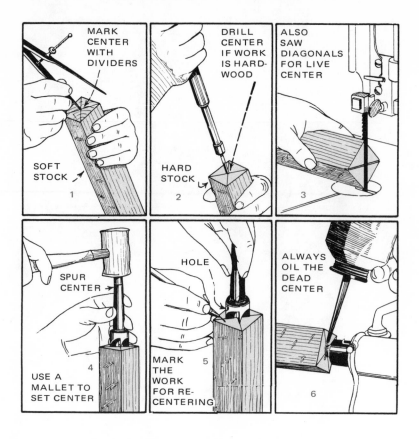

Fig. 13-2. Preparing spindle work for mounting.

stock into position. Lock the tail stock to the lathe bed and feed the cup center (sometimes called the dead center) into the stock while turning the lathe by hand. This will form a "bearing" that should be at least 1/16 in. deep. Back out the cup center, lubricate it with oil or wax and then move it back into position. Leave a very slight clearance so that the lathe turns easily. Lock the tail stock spindle clamp.

THE TOOL REST

The top of the tool rest should be smooth and free of nicks so lathe tools, Fig. 13-3 (also called chisels) can be easily moved along this surface. For most spindle turning the rest should be just slightly above the center of the work. It should clear the work by 1/8 to 1/4 in. Stop the lathe and reposition the tool

Fig. 13-3. Wood turning chisels.

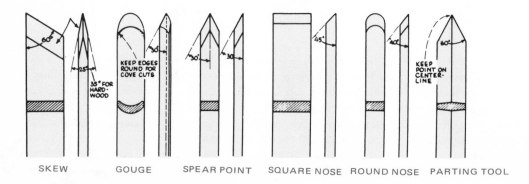

rest as the diameter of the work is reduced. Remove the tool rest when sanding or polishing the work.

SPINDLE TURNING

Set the lathe on the lowest speed and turn it by hand to see that the tool rest clears the stock. Select a large gouge and turn on the power.

Place the gouge on the tool rest holding it firmly, using the method shown in Figs. 13-4 or 13-5. By turning the gouge slightly you will be able to direct the flow of shavings to the side. Take light cuts, moving from left to right across the work until the tool cuts smoothly, indicating that a cylinder has been formed.

To turn the cylinder to a prescribed diameter, use the caliper and parting tool as shown in Fig. 13-6. The parting tool is held with the edge on the tool rest. If the cylinder is smooth and round you can place the caliper on the work while it is turning. Cut with the parting tool until the caliper just slips over the work. Space several of these cuts along the work and then use a large skew to cut down to these diameters. The parting tool can also be used to square off the ends to the required length.

The expert woodturner will use gouges and skews to make shearing cuts that result in a very smooth surface. The beginner, however, should limit his work to scraping cuts produced by holding the tools level and touching the work directly in front of the tool rest. Concave cuts are made with the round nose and convex cuts with the spear point or skew. A single beveled tool, such as the spear point, should be used with the bevel side down.

After the work is turned to a smooth cylinder you can increase the speed of the lathe. How fast you can safely turn the work will depend on its diameter. Large diameter stock must be turned at slow speed. Use good judgment as you select higher speeds, and secure advice from your instructor.

MOUNTING WORK ON FACEPLATE

When screw holes will not detract from the finished turning, the stock can be fastened directly to the faceplate. Usually, however, it is better to glue the work to a backing block.

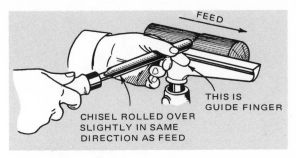

Fig. 13-4. Using a gouge to turn down a cylinder.

Fig. 13-5. Another method of holding the gouge.

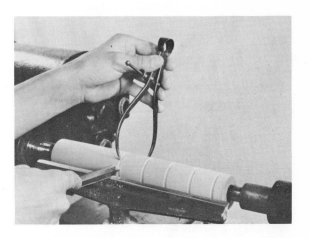

Fig. 13-6. Laying out diameters with parting tool and outside caliper.

Rough out the diameter of both the backing block and the stock for the finished turning. Check their surfaces to see that they are flat and will fit together smoothly. Spread glue on the surface of each piece, place a sheet of paper in the joint and clamp them together. Allow the glue to harden overnight, then mount the work on a faceplate, Fig. 13-7. Screw the faceplate on the lathe spindle and turn the work.

Fig. 13-7. Faceplate turning. Left. Mounting stock on faceplate. Center. Truing edge with a spear point.
Right. Using a round nose chisel.

After the turning is finished, use a wide wood chisel to split the glue line. Keep the faceplate mounted on the lathe and work carefully all the way around the joint with the bevel of the chisel turned toward the backing block.

FACEPLATE TURNING

All faceplate turning should be done by the scraping method with the tool rest holding the cutting tool edge on a level line through the center of the work. The spear point, round nose and skew are good tools to use. The gouge should not be used on faceplate work.

Screw the faceplate onto the lathe spindle until it is tight against the shoulder. Set the lathe on the slowest speed and true the edge with a shoulder cut, using the spear point as shown in Fig. 13-7. Position the tool rest along the face of the stock and make a light cut, working from the center toward the outside. When both the edge and face are smooth and true, you can increase the speed (if the diameter is not large) to finish the turning.

SANDING LATHE WORK

Work can be sanded while it is rotating in the lathe. Always remove the tool rest. Work that has been scraped will require a considerable amount of sanding. Fold the abrasive paper into a pad and hold it in your fingers. A strip of paper held by the ends will often work best for spindle turnings. Since you are actually sanding across the grain with the lathe turning, you should use a very fine paper to finish the work. Final sanding should be done by hand, with the lathe stopped and working in the direction of the wood grain.

SPECIAL CHUCKING AND MOUNTING

There are many ways to mount work in a lathe. Fig. 13-8 shows a ball foot being turned in a drill chuck. The stock was prepared by gluing a piece of 3/8 in. dowel into a section of 1 1/4 in. dowel. A square block of wood could be used instead of the 1 1/4 in. dowel.

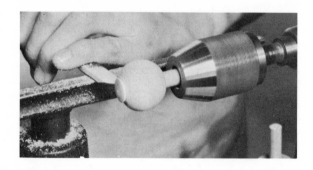

Fig. 13-8. Mounting the work in a drill chuck.

Fig. 13-9 shows the use of a "drive" chuck to mount a small part. The chuck is made by mounting a piece of hardwood on the faceplate. A 5/8 in. hole is then carefully bored through the center. Pieces of 1/2 in. square stock can be driven into the chuck. When the turning is complete, the knock-out rod (used to remove the spur center) is used to drive the piece out of the chuck.

If a drill chuck is not available to turn the ball foot, as shown in Fig. 13-8, the "drive" chuck could be used. Mount the 1/2 in. square stock, turn it to a 3/8 in. diameter, then glue on the 1 1/4 in. dowel. If the fit is tight you will need to wait only a few minutes before continuing with the work.

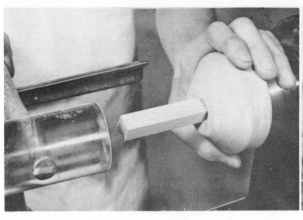

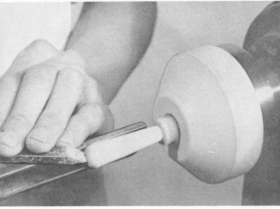

Fig. 13-9. A drive chuck. Left. Driving a 1/2 in. square into a 5/8 in. hole. Right. Turning leg for a candelabra.

Turning on a "mandrel" is shown in Fig. 13-10. Here the square stock, driven in the chuck, has been turned to a slight taper. A section of dowel with a

Fig. 13-10. Turning work mounted on a mandrel.

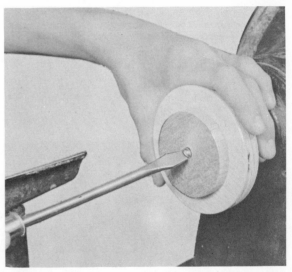

Fig.13-11. Mounting small wheel on a wood blank fastened to faceplate.

hole drilled through its center has been pressed on and is being turned. Empty thread spools can be used instead of the drilled dowels.

Small wheels for pull toys and models can be quickly mounted on the faceplate with a wood screw as shown in Fig. 13-11. The blanks are first cut out on the jig saw and then turned on the lathe; first on one side and then the other.

Small parts are fun to turn on the lathe. Always keep your tools sharp, and do a lot of shaping with coarse abrasive paper.

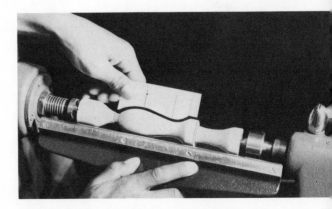

Fig. 13-12. Using a template to check contour (shape) of turning.

LATHE SAFETY RULES

SAMMY SAFETY
SAYS:

"1. Before starting the machine, be sure that spindle work has the cup center properly imbedded, tail stock and tool rest are securely clamped, and that there is proper clearance between the rotating stock and the tool rest.

2. Before starting the machine for faceplate work, check to see that the faceplate is tight against the spindle shoulder.

3. Wear goggles or a face shield to protect your eyes.

4. Select turning speed carefully. Large diameters must be turned at the lowest speed. Always use the lowest speed to rough out work.

5. Wood with knots and splits should not be turned. Glued-up stock should cure at least overnight.

6. Keep the tool rest close to the work.

7. Remove the tool rest for sanding operations.

8. Use a scraping cut for faceplate work.

9. Remove both live and dead centers when not in use.

10. When you stop the lathe to check your work also check and oil the cup center.

11. Keep the lathe tools sharp.

12. Do not wear loose sleeves or neckties. They are especially hazardous around a lathe."

QUIZ — UNIT 13

1. A 12 in. lathe will measure _____ in. from the bed to the center of the spindle.

2. When in use the tool rest assembly is clamped to the _____ of the lathe.

3. The spur center is mounted in the spindle of the _____ .

4. The turning tool that should be used for roughing out spindle work is called a _____ .

5. When using round nose turning tool, beveled side should be turned _____ .

6. Faceplate turning should be done by the _____ method.

7. A piece of paper should be placed in the glue line when mounting turning stock on a _____ .

8. When roughing out spindle work, the tool should be moved from _____ to _____ .

9. When turning the face surface of faceplate work, it is best to move the tool from the _____ toward the _____ .

10. When sanding work on the lathe, the _____ should be removed.

Left. Automatic lathe set up to produce baseball bats. Stock (mounted between centers) revolves about 25 rpm as it is moved back into the large cutterhead assembly (arrow). The cutterhead revolves at a high speed — forming the bat in just a few seconds. Above. Close-up view of cutterhead "makeup" for producing bowling pins.
(Mattison Machine Works)

WOOD, LUMBER, FOREST PRODUCTS

1. **The structure of wood and how it grows.**
2. **How wood shrinks when it is dried.**
3. **How trees are made into lumber.**
4. **How plywood, hardboard and particleboard are manufactured.**

WOOD STRUCTURE AND GROWTH

The basic structure of wood consists of long narrow tubes or cells (called fibers or tracheids) no larger around than a human hair. Their length varies from about 1/25 in. in hardwoods to about 1/4 in. in softwoods. The cell walls are composed of tiny strands of cellulose. The structure also includes cells that run in a direction from the pith to the bark and form the wood rays. All of these cells or fibers vary in size and shape and are held together with a substance called lignin.

New cells are formed in the cambium layer that is located just under the bark of the tree. The inside of this layer develops new wood cells and the outside develops new bark. The growth in the cambium layer takes place during the spring and summer and forms separate layers each year. These layers are called annular rings. See Figs. 14-1 and 14-2.

In the spring trees grow rapidly and the cells produced are large and thin walled. As the growth of the tree slows down during the summer months the cells produced are thick walled, dense and appear darker in color. These annular growth rings form the wood grain patterns that are seen on the surface of boards cut from the tree.

Fig. 14-2. Section of log showing annular rings. (Forest Products Laboratory)

The sapwood contains living cells and may be several inches or more in thickness. Faster growing trees usually have a thicker layer of sapwood. The heartwood of the tree is formed as the sapwood cells become inactive. It usually has a darker color because of the presence of gums and resins.

MOISTURE CONTENT AND SHRINKAGE

Before wood can be used, a large part of the moisture (sap) must be removed. When a living tree is cut, more than half of its weight may be moisture. The heartwood of a "green" birch tree has a moisture

Fig. 14-1. Parts of a tree trunk.

content of about 75 percent. Most cabinet and furniture woods are dried to a moisture content of 6 to 10 percent.

The amount of moisture in wood is expressed as a percent of the oven-dry weight of the wood. For example; a piece of wood that weight 12 lbs. was completely dried in an oven and was then found to weigh 10 lbs. The amount of moisture in the original piece was 2 lbs. or 20 percent of the oven-dry weight.

Moisture in wood is contained in the cell cavities and in the cell walls. As lumber dries, the moisture first leaves the cell cavities. When the cells are empty but the cell walls are still full of moisture, the wood has reached a condition called the fiber saturation point. This is at about 30 percent moisture content for all kinds of wood.

Wood does not start to shrink until after the fiber saturation point has been reached. If dried to a 15 percent moisture content, it will have been reduced by about one half of the total shrinkage possible. A plain sawn birch board that was 12 in. wide at 30 percent moisture content will measure only about 11 in. at 0 percent moisture content. Wood shrinks most along the direction of the annular rings and a little less across these rings. There is practically no shrinkage in the length. How this shrinkage affects lumber cut from a log is shown in Fig. 14-3. As moisture is added to wood, it swells in the same proportion that the shrinkage has taken place.

A piece of wood will give off or take on moisture from the air around it until the moisture in the wood is balanced with that in the air. At this point the wood is said to be at equilibrium moisture content (E.M.C.). Since wood is exposed to daily and seasonal changes in the relative humidity of the air, it is continually making slight changes in its moisture content and, therefore, changes in its dimensions. This is the reason doors and drawers often stick during humid summer months but work freely the rest of the year.

Moisture change in wood takes place slowly under normal conditions. Paint and other finishes will slow the action still more but will not entirely prevent it. An article should be made of wood that has a moisture content very close to the E.M.C. it will attain in service. Try to design your projects so that the shrinking and swelling of the wood will not affect the structure.

LUMBERING

The method and equipment used in lumbering vary according to the geographic location and the size of the operation. In general, however, lumbering includes selecting and cutting the trees, Fig. 14-4, transporting the logs to the sawmill, sawing the logs into lumber and drying and planing the lumber.

The lumbering industry moved across the continent with the pioneers. It has grown with the nation and today is our fifth largest industry. There are many sawmills, some in every state, that provide lumber to about 4,000 wholesalers, who, in turn, supply some 30,000 retail lumber yards. The development of heavy machines and equipment, plus continued improvement in methods and procedures, has resulted in a high level of efficiency. Today, for the nation as a whole, it takes only about 28 man-hours to log, manufacture and distribute to the consumer a thousand board feet of lumber.

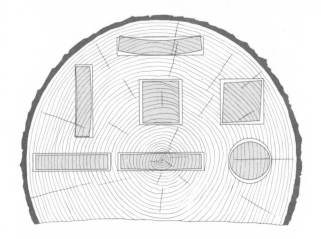

Fig. 14-3. How wood shrinks.
(Forest Products Laboratory)

Our forests are one of our greatest national resources. The trees that supply lumber and other forest products are a "crop" that can be grown over and over again on the same land. Through sound management under the American Tree Farm System millions of acres of woodlands are being protected and managed so that our wood supply can last indefinitely. About 42 percent of our lumber comes from industry owned lands. Privately owned land, including farm wood lots, provide about 48 percent, with the remaining 10 percent coming from land owned by the government.

Today scientific studies are used to select the timber and method of cutting. After the tree is cut down and trimmed, it is cut into suitable lengths. The logs are then skidded to a central point, where they are loaded on trucks or railroad cars for the trip to the sawmill. In a few areas, logs are floated down

In large mills, logs are pulled up a "jack ladder" to the sawing deck where they are washed and the bark is removed, Fig. 14-6. The log is then placed on the carriage of the "headrig" and moved through a giant band saw that cuts the log into boards and timbers, Fig. 14-7.

Fig. 14-4. Left. Power chain saw bites through tree 10 times faster than hand operated saw. Fig. 14-5. Center. Logs arriving at mill are stored in pond. Fig. 15-6. Right. Stream of water of a pressure of 1350 pounds per square inch removes bark from log. (Weyehaeuser Co.)

rivers or streams to the mill. At the sawmill the logs are usually stored in ponds, Fig. 14-5, until they can be sawed. The water makes it easy to move and sort the logs and prevents end checking. Some hardwood logs are too heavy to float very well, and are stacked in the mill yard where they are sprayed with water to keep them from drying out.

From the headrig the boards move to smaller edger and trimmer saws that cut them to proper widths and lengths. The boards are then sorted, graded and stacked either in open sheds for air drying, or in huge ovens for kiln drying, Fig. 14-8. Large mills have a planing mill section where the dried lumber is surfaced and made into finished lumber, Fig. 14-9.

Fig. 14-7. Left. Headrig rips log into boards. Band saw blade (see arrow) is over 60 ft. long. Fig. 14-8. Center. Moving wood into dry kiln. Notice "stickers" that separate the layers so air can move around each piece. Fig. 14-9. Right. Planing lumber to specified dimensions. Two inch lumber can be S4S at the rate of 600 linear feet per minute.
(American Forest Prod. Ind.)   (Forest Products Lab.)   (Weyerhaeuser Co.)

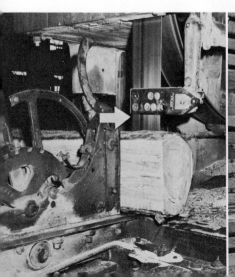 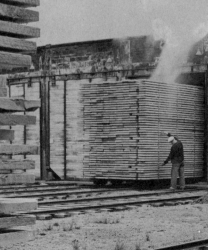 

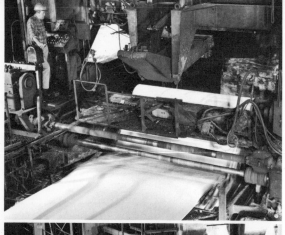

Fig. 14-10. Top. Rotary cutting veneer. Fig. 14-11. Center. Veneer sheets move from dryer to revolving table for sorting. Fig. 14-12. Bottom. Applying glue and stacking veneer sheets. (American Plywood Assoc.)

PLYWOOD

Many top-quality logs are made into plywood. The veneer is produced either by sawing, slicing or rotary cutting, Fig. 14-10. In rotary cutting, the most common method, the logs are mounted in a large lathe and are rotated against a razor-sharp knife that peels off a thin continuous sheet of wood. The long sheet of veneer is cut into specific widths and is then run through a dryer, Fig. 14-11, to remove the moisture.

The sheets are carefully sorted and matched so that the best veneers will be on the outside of the plywood. They are then coated with glue, Fig. 14-12, and stacked so that the grain of each sheet is at a right angle to that of the next. The stacks are placed in powerful presses that exert a pressure of more than 150 lbs. per square inch. The plates of the press are heated to speed the setting of the glue. After the panels leave the presses, they are sanded and trimmed to size.

HARDBOARD

Hardboard is a manufactured product made from wood fibers. The fibers can be secured from any kind of wood. Shavings and small pieces (formerly considered to be waste material) are often utilized.

The wood is first reduced to individual fibers, either by a steam process or mechanical grinding. The fibers are thoroughly washed, Fig. 14-15. They are then mixed with water and fed onto a moving screen. The water runs through the screen and a thick blanket of fibers is formed, Fig. 14-16.

The blanket is pressed between rollers and cut into sheets. These sheets are then placed in giant hot presses where the lignin (natural adhesive in wood) bonds the fibers together into hard, stiff boards.

Hardboard panels are usually 1/8, 3/16 and 1/4 in. thick. Various textures can be molded into the surface or designs can be cut through the material. Hardboard is often finished with a printed wood grain pattern, Fig. 14-17. Panels with this type of finish are widely used for wall paneling and furniture construction.

PARTICLEBOARD

Particleboard is made from wood flakes and chips, bonded together with an adhesive. The manufacturing process includes many of the same operations used to make hardboard, Fig. 14-18. Particleboard is not as dense (heavy) as hardboard. After the panels are formed the surfaces are usually sanded.

Particleboard can be made with different sizes of chips. Large chips are generally used in the center to provide strength and fine ones at the surface to provide smoothness. Thicknesses may range from 1/4 to over 1 inch.

Fig. 14-13. After the veneers are laid up, they are placed between platens (steel plates) of a giant press. Pressure and heat are then applied and the veneers are bonded together, forming plywood panels.   (American Plywood Assoc.)

Fig. 14-14. Plywood panels are run through giant power sanders as a final operation in making "wood-and-glue sandwiches" ready for the market.   (American Plywood Assoc.)

Fig. 14-15. Giant washing machines clean wood fiber stock that will be used to make hardboard.
(Masonite Corp.)

Today, particleboard panels are often used as a substitute for plywood. It is satisfactory for all kinds of unexposed (inside) construction in furniture making and cabinetwork. Some plywood panels have a particleboard core (center). Particleboard is a good material to use for table and counter tops when the surface is covered with a plastic laminate. It can be worked with regular woodworking tools.

Fig. 14-16. Technician checks thickness of wood fiber blanket (machine has been stopped). This four inch blanket will be compressed into a hardboard panel 1/4 in. thick.
(Masonite Corp.)

Fig. 14-17. Modern graining machine (off-set process) prints wood-grain pattern on hardboard panels. Each set of rollers apply a slightly different color – producing an appearance very similar to real wood. (International Paper Co.)

Fig. 14-18. Particleboard is bonded into panels in this giant multi-platen (plate) press. All mechanisms are controlled by a single operator (arrow) stationed at a console.
(Georgia-Pacific Corp.)

HOW WE USE LUMBER

Lumber production in the United States increases each year. The Department of Commerce predicts that the demand for wood products will double by the year 2000. Our current annual production of forest products requires about 12 billion cubic feet of wood.

Most of our lumber is used to build homes, public and commercial buildings and other large frame structures. Four out five of our homes are built with wood frames, Fig. 14-19. Wood is used for outside and inside finish. The soft, warm tones, and interesting textures and grain patterns make it an ideal material for doors, casings, cabinets and built-in fixtures. Wood is easy to cut and shape and lasts a long time.

Fig. 14-19. Most of the lumber used in this country goes into the construction of homes and industrial buildings.
(Weyerhaeuser Co.)

Most hardwood lumber goes to industrial plants that produce furniture, case and cabinet work, boats, parts for machinery, athletic equipment and many other articles that make our work easier and our lives more enjoyable.

One of many new developments that extends the use we make of lumber is the prefabrication of trusses, arches and other structural units by glued lamination. Lamination of wood, coupled with specially designed metal connectors, has become an important element in both light and heavy construction.

OTHER PRODUCTS OF THE FOREST

Wood is about 50 percent pure cellulose, and through the magic of modern chemistry it can be made into thousands of products. Some of the more important ones are paints and lacquers, photographic film, cellophane, rayon, plastics, linoleum, alcohol and resins.

Each year more than 15 million cords of pulp wood and tremendous amounts of wood residue (waste) are used for paper and cardboard. Books, newspapers, magazines, packages for food products, shipping boxes and countless other items are products of our forests.

QUIZ — UNIT 14

1. Wood cells or fibers are held together with a substance called _____ .
2. Wood cells are formed in a layer under the bark called _____ .
3. After a tree is cut down its age can be determined by counting the _____ _____ .
4. If a piece of wood that weighed 55 grams was thoroughly oven-dried and then found to weigh 50 grams, the moisture content would have been _____ percent.
5. The fiber saturation point for all kinds of wood is about _____ percent moisture content.
6. The abbreviation E.M.C. stands for _____ .
7. Today, with modern methods and equipment, it takes about _____ man-hours to produce a thousand board feet of lumber.
8. The two methods of drying lumber are air drying and _____ drying.
9. The most common method of cutting veneer is the _____ method.
10. Plywood panels are formed in giant presses that apply both _____ and pressure.

Fig. 14-20. Central control panel for a modern papermaking machine. The machine is over 400 ft. long. The paper mat is formed through a process similar to the one used to produce the hardboard blanket described on page 90. It is then dried by running it over as many as 50 heated rolls. Note the giant roll of paper being produced (arrow). (Westvaco Corp.)

CAREER OPPORTUNITIES

1. **Forestry work.**

2. **Lumbering operations.**

3. **Woodworking trades.**

4. **Wood science and research.**

Many occupations are avilable to persons who are interested in woodworking. They range from the cultivation of trees; to cutting lumber and making plywood; to fabrication of furniture and cabinetwork; to the distribution and sales of products. Employment opportunities are provided by more than 50,000 manufacturing plants, a vast distribution system, and some 75,000 builders and contractors.

FORESTRY

Careers in forestry consist of important and exciting work. Basically, they deal with the management of our forests so that the nations supply of timber will be continuous. Many specialists are needed in the areas of planting and cultivation, disease and pest control, fire protection, selection and cutting, and recreational planning. See Fig. 15-1.

Professional foresters are trained in environmental matters. They know how to maintain a continuous supply of raw material and, at the same time protect the soil, water, air and wildlife. You can obtain booklets that tell about careers in forestry by writing to The Forest Service, U.S. Department of Agriculture, Washington, D.C., 20250.

LUMBERING

The United States produces one-third of the world's lumber, over one-half of its plywood and nearly one-half of its paper and paper board. Lumbering operations begin with the selection and cutting of trees, Fig. 15-2. After the logs arrive at the sawmill, many skilled operators and technicians are needed to change it into lumber, plywood, composition board, and many other materials. See Figs. 15-3, 15-4 and UNIT 14.

MANUFACTURING

Industrial woodworking plants convert the lumber, plywood and other basic forest products into furniture, doors, windows, and many other finished products, Fig. 15-5. Today, an increasing number of plants specialize in the manufacture of building components (units). Thus the construction industry is provided with "parts" instead of "pieces" which reduces labor costs at the building site.

Woodworking plants provide employment for unskilled and semiskilled workers, where only a few weeks of training is required. These jobs include

Fig. 15-1. Foresters graft a scion (budded shoot) from a superior tree to a tree in a seed orchard. This is one of many steps used to develop "supertrees" that will grow nearly twice as fast as naturally grown trees. (Georgia-Pacific)

Fig. 15-2. Here is an exciting job — felling (cutting) trees. One logger makes the backcut with a modern chain saw. The other logger drives a steel wedge into the kerf to relieve pressure on the saw chain. (Weyerhaeuser Co.)

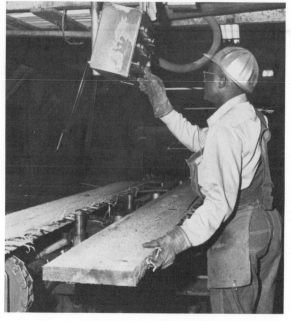

Fig. 15-3. Skilled workman operates control panel of conveyor lines in a modern sawmill. These conveyor lines move rough sawn boards from headrig to edger and trimmer saws. (International Paper Co.)

Fig. 15-4. Technician performs final inspection of plywood. Conveyor line mechanism turns panel over so both sides can be checked. Panels are then automatically stacked by equipment shown in foreground.

Fig. 15-5. Basic assembly of chest of drawers in a furniture factory. The units are then placed on a conveyor line that carries them through additional assembly operations and finishing.   (Thomasville Furniture Ind. Inc.)

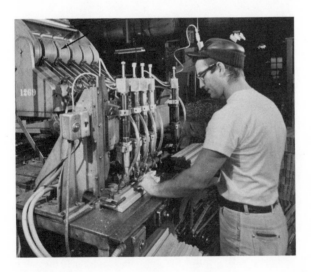

Fig. 15-6. Multiple screw driving machine attaches hardware to window jamb. Screws are automatically fed from hoppers (arrow).   (Caradco)

feeding machines and handling material, Fig. 15-6. The increasing use of automatic equipment is reducing the need for unskilled workers.

More important job opportunities consist of setting up machines, grinding cutter knives, and checking adjustments during production. These jobs require skilled craftsmen with lots of experience. Technical training is required to qualify for the work of

building machine fixtures, organizing production lines, and directing the production schedule.

Other woodworking occupations include boatbuilding wood finishing and patternmaking. The latter consists of making the wooden models used in metal casting. Most of the workers in these areas must be highly skilled. Technical training (secured in school or on the job) will usually result in rapid advancement.

CONSTRUCTION

Experts predict that the construction industry will grow very rapidly in the next few years, and will continue to require a higher proportion of skilled workers than any of the manufacturing industries.

Approximately one-third of all building construction craftsmen are carpenters — the largest single skilled occupation. Carpenters are key workers on the construction site and must know the where, when and how of nearly every kind of building material. Their work includes many types of construction — residential (homes), commercial, industrial and institutional buildings.

The carpenter must be highly skilled in the use of tools and machines. Many of the hand tools are just like the ones you have learned about in the school shop. See Fig. 15-7.

To become a skilled carpenter (called a "journeyman"), you need to complete high school or technical school courses. Then, you must serve as an apprentice for a number of years, learning information and skills on the job. An apprentice receives wages ranging from 50 to 90 percent of a journeyman carpenter.

A career as a carpenter is hard work, but it also is profitable and interesting. Carpenters experience a special feeling of satisfaction at the end of each day or week — as they see the results of their efforts.

DISTRIBUTION

Many career opportunities exist in the distribution and sale of lumber and wood products. There are over 30,000 retail building supply centers in the nation. To find employment in these centers you must have a good understanding of wood and building materials. You must be able to read blueprints, prepare estimates and figure building costs. It will also be helpful

Fig. 15-7. Carpenter hanging (installing) an interior door. Note the spiral ratchet screwdriver he is using to attach a hinge.   (Stanley Tools)

Fig. 15-8. Wood scientist injects radioactive isotopes into growing container. A radiation counter is then used to detect the movement of nutritional elements within the tree — one small part of the search for ways to grow better trees faster. (Weyerhaeuser Co.)

if you have a general knowledge of application procedures (how materials are put together).

Managers and salesmen in furniture stores should be able to identify various kinds of wood. They also need to know about wood joints, types of construction, and kinds and qualities of wood finishes.

WOOD SCIENCE AND TECHNOLOGY

Industrial companies and government agencies offer attractive career opportunities to wood scientists and technologists. Each day the search continues for better methods of growing trees; ways to make greater use of wood waste; and more efficient manufacturing processes. See Fig. 15-8. Wood scientists need a high level of technical knowledge. This is also true for those who design and build woodworking machines, compound adhesives and develop new wood finishes.

College and university degrees are generally required for those who work in forestry, forest product research, and furniture and cabinet design. More than 40 schools located throughout the nation provide training in this field of study.

If you have ability in woodwork and enjoy working with young people, the teaching profession can offer you a rewarding career. Over 200 educational institutions (some in every state) offer teaching degrees in Industrial Arts and Technical subjects. Ask your instructor about opportunities in teaching as well as those in the various areas of woodworking.

For information about careers in woodworking, write to:

Director
Wood Industry Careers Program
National Forest Products Association
1619 Massachusetts Avenue
Washington D.C. 20036

WOODWORKING PROJECTS

1. **Complete project plans.**

2. **Working drawings without plans of procedure.**

3. **Project photos and brief descriptions.**

On the following pages you will find a number of projects that you may want to build. Complete plans are provided for the first two. Even though you do not build these particular projects you will benefit from a study of them. They show you how drawings are made and how plans of procedure and bills of material are set up.

The second group provides a working drawing and you will need to prepare the plan of procedure and bill of material. Some helpful suggestions concerning the procedure are given.

The last group shows a picture along with a brief written description and you will need to develop all the planning materials.

Your work in the shop will not be limited to these projects and they are presented only as examples of what can be done. You will find many other good ideas for projects in magazines and catalogs and in stores and homes.

TRINKET BOX

The handy little box, Fig. 16-1, can be used to hold all kinds of small items. Its construction involves some important hand tool and gluing operations which can be applied to numerous other projects.

You can be sure of having good joints if you make and use the jigs and setups shown in the instructional pictures on rabbet joints and grooves.

After the basic box is built, you may want to apply your own ideas to the design. The corners could be chamfered or rounded and other curves cut along the bottom edge. Small blocks or turnings can

be attached to the bottom for feet. You might want to add a simple carving, inlay or overlay to the top.

The inside of the box can be lined with felt or divided into compartments. To use a felt or fabric lining, first cut pieces of cardboard slightly smaller than the inside surfaces. Attach the material by cutting it larger than the cardboard, and then turning it over the edges and gluing it to the back side. The covered pieces of cardboard are then glued in place. If you line the box you may want to use hinges to attach the top.

PLAN OF PROCEDURE FOR TRINKET BOX

(See Figs. 16-1, 16-2 and 16-3)

1. Make a stock-cutting list.
2. Select the material and rough it out.
3. Plane one side of the stock for the inside surface.
4. Plane the stock for the sides and ends to finished width.
5. Cut the sides and ends to finished length.
6. Square the bottom to finished size.
7. Cut the groove for the bottom, in the sides and ends. (If this operation is performed on the power saw, it should be done while the stock is in one piece.)
8. Cut the rabbet joints in the sides.
9. Make a trial assembly of the sides, ends and bottom. Trim and fit the joints as required.
10. Sand the inside surfaces of the sides and ends and both surfaces of the bottom.
11. Glue up the bottom, sides and ends.
12. Fit the top to the sides and ends.
13. Sand the inside surface of the top and glue it in place.
14. Plane all outside surfaces.

Fig. 16-1. Trinket box you can make.

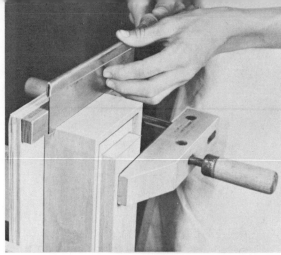

Fig. 16-3. Using a jig as a guide to cut the box open. Similar cuts are made on all four sides.

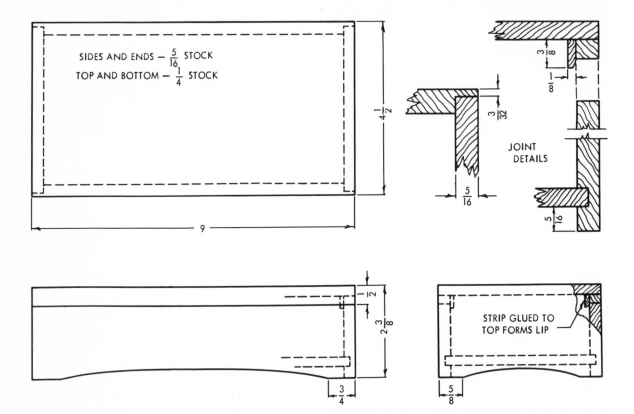

SIDES AND ENDS — $\frac{5}{16}$ STOCK

TOP AND BOTTOM — $\frac{1}{4}$ STOCK

JOINT DETAILS

STRIP GLUED TO TOP FORMS LIP

Fig. 16-2. Trinket box, working drawing.

15. Cut off the lid and plane and sand the edge.
16. Cut, fit and glue in the strip that forms the lip.
17. Cut and sand the contours on the bottom edges.
18. Prepare all surfaces for finish.
19. Seal all surfaces and sand down.
20. Apply two coats of varnish to outside surfaces. Sand between coats.
21. Polish and wax.

BILL OF MATERIAL FOR THE TRINKET BOX

NO.	SIZE	KIND	PART
1 pc.	1/4 x 4 1/4 x 9	Basswood	Top
1 pc.	1/4 x 4 3/16 x 8 11/16	Basswood	Bottom
2 pcs.	5/16 x 2 3/8 x 9	Basswood	Sides
2 pcs.	5/16 x 2 3/8 x 4 5/16	Basswood	Ends
1 pc.	1/8 x 3/8 x 26	Basswood	Lip

Finish as required

BOOKRACK

A bookrack, as shown in Fig. 16-4 or Fig. 16-5, will be a good one to have on your desk at home. Since it is so easy to remove or replace a book with this type of rack, it should be reserved for books that are used a great deal. Select a kind of wood and finish that will go with the other room furnishings.

If this is your first experience in woodwork, it will probably be best for you to follow closely the plans and drawings. You will find a number of instructional pictures showing operations being performed on the bookrack, in the units on hand woodwork.

This type of bookrack, sometimes called a book ramp, can be made in many different ways. The experienced student may want to change the size and design. Tapering the base as well as the upright takes more work but gives a pleasing effect.

PLAN OF PROCEDURE FOR THE BOOKRACK

(See Figs. 16-4, 16-5 and 16-6)

1. Make a stock-cutting list.
2. Select and rough out the stock.

Fig. 16-4. Completed bookrack.

Fig. 16-5. Bookrack, alternate design.

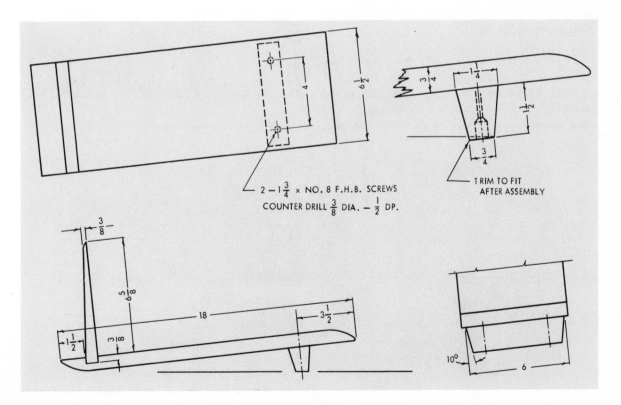

Fig. 16-6. Bookrack, working drawing.

3. Make the base and upright.
   a. Surface the stock on both faces, using a hand plane with the grain.
   b. Plane to finished width.
   c. Square off one end, lay out and plane the taper for the upright.
   d. Cut off the upright and square the base to finished length.
4. Lay out and cut the dado joint that joins the upright to the base.
5. Make the shoe.
   a. Glue up the required thickness.
   b. Plane the stock to finished thickness and width.
   c. Cut the shoe to finished length and at the required angle.
   d. Plane the angle on the sides.
6. Attach the shoe to the base.
   a. Clamp the shoe into position.
   b. Lay out and drill the screw holes.
   c. Set the screws.
   d. Plane the bottom of the shoe to fit.
7. Assemble the upright in the base and make any adjustments.
8. Disassemble the project and round the ends of the base and upright.
9. Sand all parts and prepare them for finish.
10. Glue the upright in place and attach the shoe.
11. Check all surfaces and resand if necessary.
12. Apply the wood finish.
    a. Apply paste filler, if required.
    b. Seal all surfaces.
    c. Sand the sealer coat.
    d. Apply two coats of finish. Sand lightly between coats.
    e. Polish and wax.

BILL OF MATERIAL FOR THE BOOKRACK

NO.	SIZE	KIND	PART
1 pc.	3/4 x 6 1/2 x 18	Ash	Base
1 pc.	3/4 x 6 1/2 x 7	Ash	Upright
1 pc.	1 1/4 x 1 1/2 x 6	Ash	Shoe
2 — 1 3/4 x No. 8 F.H.B. wood screws			

CUBE LAMP

For the cube lamp base, select a soft textured wood with an interesting grain pattern. The large globe-like bulb is available at most hardware or electrical stores. See Fig. 16-7.

Lay out one piece of stock that will make all four sides. Be sure to allow extra length for trimming and saw kerfs. After planing the surfaces and edges to the required size, cut the rabbet joint. You can use the rabbet plane, Fig. 4-7, page 24, or the circular saw,

Fig. 16-8. Cutting a rabbet with the dado head.

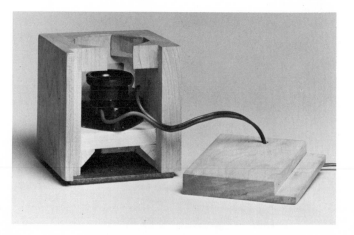

Fig. 16-7. Left. Cube lamp assembly. Right. Lamp base with side removed.

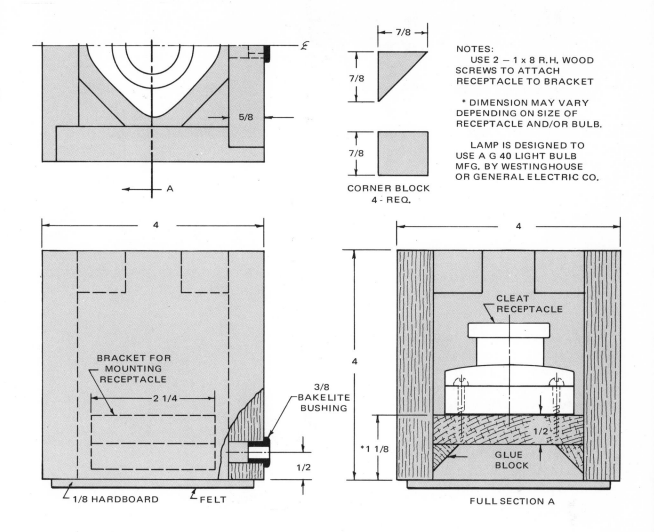

NOTES:
USE 2 — 1 x 8 R.H. WOOD
SCREWS TO ATTACH
RECEPTACLE TO BRACKET

* DIMENSION MAY VARY
DEPENDING ON SIZE OF
RECEPTACLE AND/OR BULB.

LAMP IS DESIGNED TO
USE A G 40 LIGHT BULB
MFG. BY WESTINGHOUSE
OR GENERAL ELECTRIC CO.

CORNER BLOCK
4 - REQ.

BRACKET FOR
MOUNTING
RECEPTACLE

3/8
BAKELITE
BUSHING

1/8 HARDBOARD   FELT

CLEAT
RECEPTACLE

GLUE
BLOCK

FULL SECTION A

Fig. 16-9. Working drawing of cube lamp.

Fig. 12-13, page 69. If you are mass producing the lamp, a dado head setup will save time. See Fig. 16-8.

Cut the four sides to the exact length and glue them together. Install the glue blocks as a separate operation.

Fig. 16-7, Right, shows the interior assembly of the cube lamp. It will help you understand the working drawing, Fig. 16-9. Since receptacles vary in size and shape, it is best to first attach the receptacle to the bracket. Screw in the bulb, then position this assembly in the base. With the bulb in proper position, set the glue blocks.

Apply finishing coats before installing the lamp cord, bushing, switch and plug. Attach felt to the hardboard base with glue or double-faced tape.

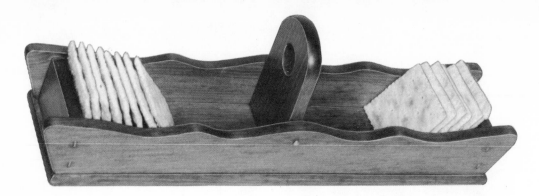

Fig. 16-10. Cracker tray.

CRACKER TRAY

It is best to use solid stock for all the parts of this project, Fig. 16-10. The sides however, could be made from 1/4 in. plywood. Resawing nominal 1 in. stock is an economical way to produce the 5/16 in. thickness. See Fig. 12-12, page 69.

Plane a smooth surface on the stock and then cut out the various parts. Draw the half pattern for the sides and make the layout as shown in Fig. 5-4. After cutting out the top contour of the sides, the edges can be sanded as shown in Fig. 16-12.

To assemble the project, first glue and nail the sides to the ends. After the glue has set, check over this subassembly carefully and then attach it to the base. The handle is installed last.

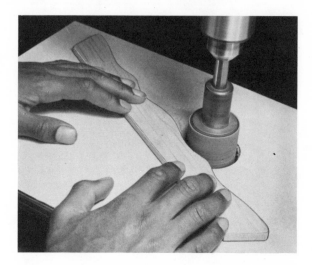

Fig. 16-12. Using a small drum sander mounted on the drill press. Be sure to use the lowest speed. An auxiliary table has been attached to the regular table.

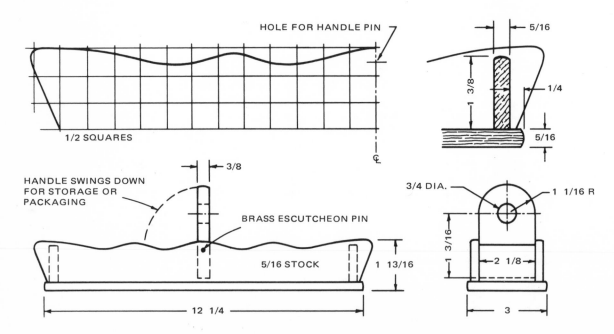

HOLE FOR HANDLE PIN

1/2 SQUARES

5/16

3/8

1

1/4

5/16

HANDLE SWINGS DOWN FOR STORAGE OR PACKAGING

3/8

BRASS ESCUTCHEON PIN

5/16 STOCK

1 13/16

12 1/4

3/4 DIA.

1 1/16 R

1 3/16

2 1/8

3

Fig. 16-11. Cracker tray, working drawing.

NAPKIN HOLDER

Cut the grooves in the base square with the surface. The slight angle (about 3 degrees) of the sides will tend to lock them in place when the parts are assembled.

When making the assembly, first insert the dowels so the sides are spaced about the same as the grooves. Apply a small amount of glue in the grooves and at the end of the dowels. Place the sides in the grooves and then force them out along the dowels with wedges. See Fig. 16-15.

Fig. 16-15. Using hardboard wedges (arrows) to hold the sides in position until the glue sets.

If this project is mass produced, cut the base material in a long strip and then form the grooves and side chamfer before cutting to length.

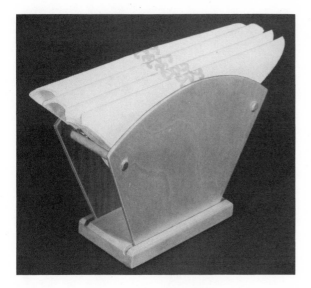

Fig. 16-13. Napkin holder.

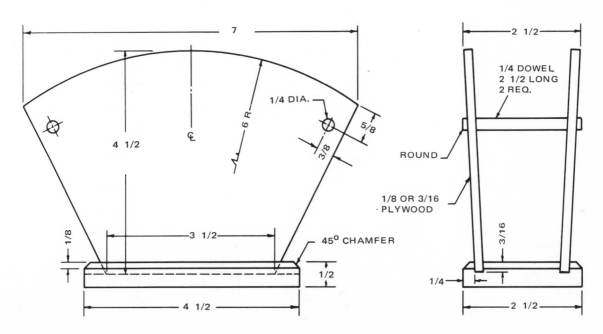

Fig. 16-14. Napkin holder, working drawing.

Fig. 16-16. Bridge set.

BRIDGE SET

Prepare the sides by first planing a strip of stock to exactly 1/2 x 3/4 inches. Carefully cut the miter joints, using a miter box. See Fig. 4-12, page 26. The length of the center spacer should be cut to fit after the sides have been assembled.

Assembling miter joints is a bit "tricky," so use a miter-frame clamp, Fig. 16-18, or a special gluing jig. The bottom should be cut out and attached after the upper frame unit has been completed. Turn and attach the handle as a final operation.

Assembly of the top frame can be simplified by using edge joints as shown in the working drawing.

Fig. 16-18. Using a miter-frame clamp to assemble the sides and ends.

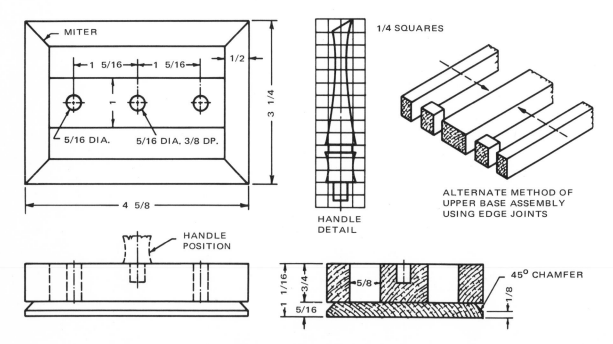

Fig. 16-17. Bridge set, working drawing.

COASTER SET

Cut square blanks for the coasters, Fig. 16-19, from stock that has been planed to 7/16 in. thick. Mark the exact center of the squares and bore a 1 in. hole — 7/32 in. deep.

Next, lay out and cut the outside contour on the jig saw. If you would prefer a beveled edge, try tilting the table, Fig. 11-8, page 61. After the coaster shapes are complete, lay out and build the rack. Glue a disk of sheet cork to the bottom of the coaster recess after the finish has been applied.

Fig. 16-19. Coaster set.

Turn a special chuck on the faceplate of the lathe as shown in Fig. 16-21. Mount the coaster blank in the chuck with a heavy gage wood screw. Use a square nose or spear point turning tool to enlarge the recess to the required diameter.

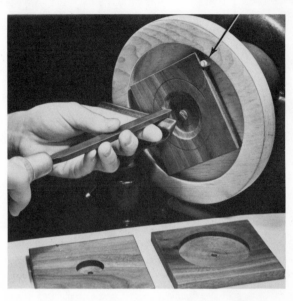

Fig. 16-21. Enlarging the coaster recess on the lathe. Note the dowel (arrow) that drives the workpiece. Keep turning speeds under 1000 rpm.

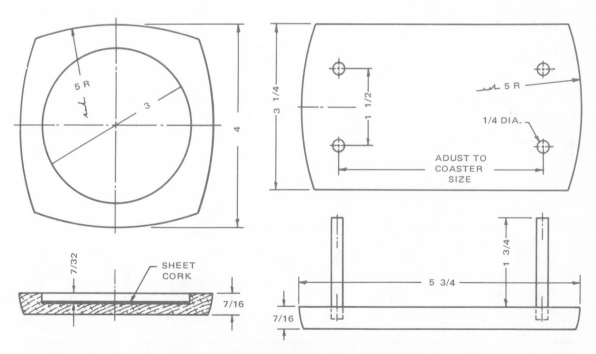

Fig. 16-20. Coaster set, working drawing.

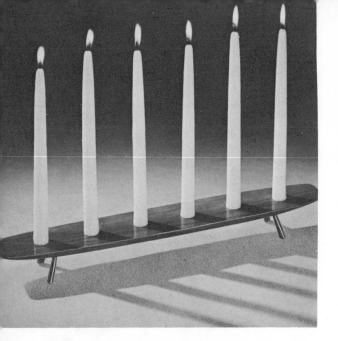

Fig. 16-22. Candelabra.

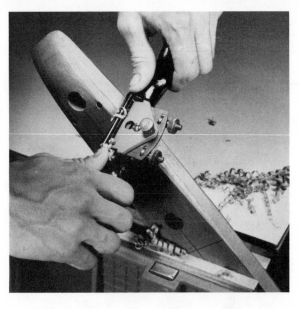

Fig. 16-24. Using a spokeshave to shape and smooth the edges and bottom.

CANDELABRA

The candelabra, Fig. 16-22, is an attractive piece for a dining or buffet setting, or for the mantle during a holiday season.

Square up the base to overall sizes and lay out and bore the holes before cutting out the contour and shaping the edges. The candelabra is shown under construction in several of the instructional pictures in the unit on drilling and boring holes. Study Fig. 6-8, page 35 before drilling holes for the legs.

The legs are turned on a lathe using the procedure shown in Fig. 13-9, page 75. If a lathe is not available, you can use wood dowels.

Give a lot of attention to shaping the curves and edges so they will be smooth and trim. See Fig. 16-24. An added touch can be gained by fitting short sections of brass tubing into the holes to hold the candles.

The attractiveness of a project like the candelabra depends a great deal on the beauty of the wood.

Fig. 16-23. Candelabra, working drawing.

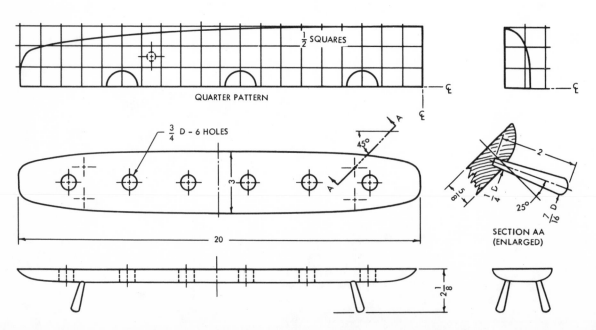

QUARTER PATTERN

$\frac{3}{4}$ D - 6 HOLES

SECTION AA
(ENLARGED)

Fig. 16-25. Spoon rack.

Fig. 16-27. Drilling holes in holder strips. Note tape (arrow) that holds workpieces together.

SPOON RACK

This Early American spoon rack is designed to hold small souvenir spoons, Fig. 16-25. First develop half patterns and then lay them out on each side of a centerline and even with an edge or line, Fig. 5-4, page 28.

The three holder strips should first be squared to size and then fastened together. This will save time in drilling the holes and cutting the slots. Wrapping each end with several layers of drafting tape will usually provide enough holding power. See Fig. 16-27.

Fasten the sides to the holder strips and then mount this assembly on the back. If you plan to use a brush to apply the finish, make this final assembly after the finishing steps are complete.

Fig. 16-26. Spoon rack, working drawing.

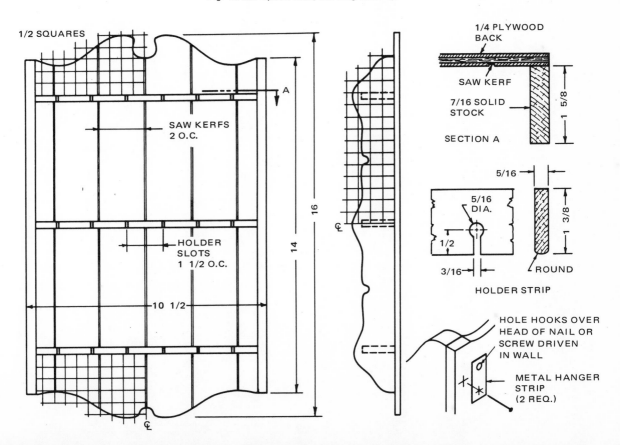

Fig. 16-28. Stool.

Fig. 16-30. Sawing off legs of stool.

STOOL

Plane and square the top to finished size and then lay out the position of the holes. These can be bored by hand, using a jig, or a drill press can be used, as shown in Fig. 11-4, page 59.

After the legs are glued in place they should be trimmed to the same length, then the bottoms should be cut off, so they will rest flat on the floor, Fig. 16-30. To do this, make a jig by boring a large hole in a piece of 3/8 in. stock. Clamp the jig to the bench top, set one leg of the stool in the hole and cut it off as shown in the picture. As each leg is cut off, use a block the same thickness as the jig (plus the saw kerf) to support it until all the cuts are made.

Fig. 16-29. Stool, working drawing.

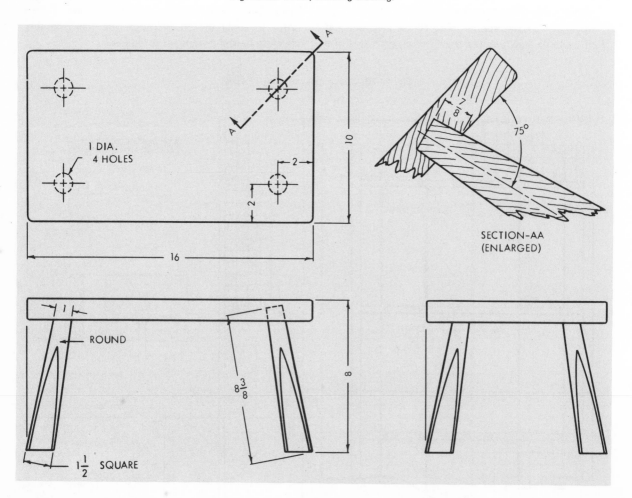

100

Fig. 16-31. Early American Tray.

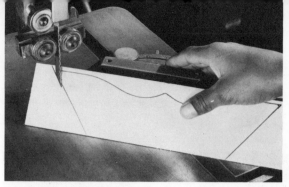

Fig. 16-33. Cutting corner joints on band saw. Workpiece is held against beveled block attached to miter gage.

EARLY AMERICAN TRAY

Use white pine for this attractive project, Fig. 16-31. It will be easy to work and is the kind of wood often used by Colonial craftsmen.

After ripping and planing the strip for the sides, plane the bevel for the bottom edge. The corner joints (called compound miters) are difficult to cut. A good procedure is to first make a beveled block that will support the sides at a 45 degree angle. This block can be placed in a miter box or attached to the miter gage of the band saw. See Fig. 16-33.

Build a jig to assemble the sides. It will be easier to make the assembly with the sides in an inverted

Fig. 16-32. Early American tray, working drawing.

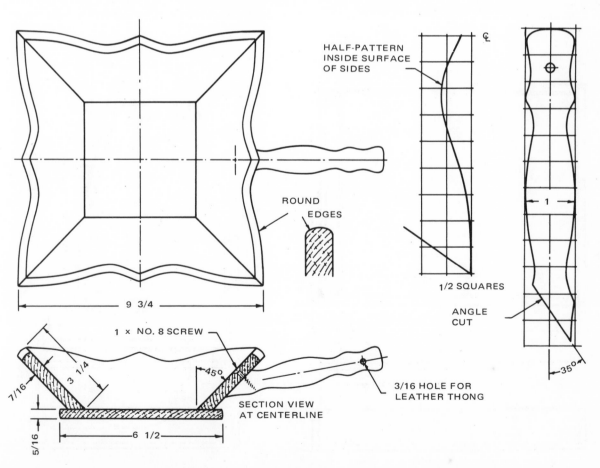

position. Try attaching four blocks to a flat surface so the corners will be held together. Then, by applying downward pressure with some type of clamp or a weight, the joints will be pressed together. The bottom and handle are attached in separate assembly operations.

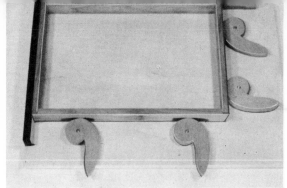

Fig. 16-36. Jig which makes it easy to glue the file box together. The eccentrics can be developed by using a string wrapped around a pencil held at the center point.

LETTER FILE AND EASEL

A letter file and easel, as shown in Fig. 16-34, serves a dual purpose. It may be used as a flat file for holding letters, bills and other papers, and can also be used as an easel to hold typing copy or a book. The picture shows how the lid and handle are placed on the sides of the box to form an easel.

Build the file box first. The rabbet for the bottom should be cut on the circular saw or with the rabbet plane while the sides and ends are in one or two long strips. They are then squared to length and the corner

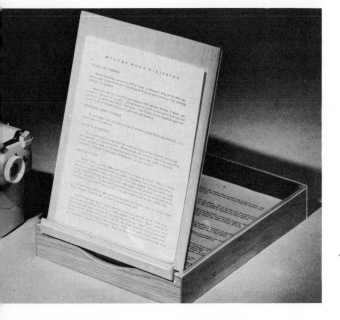

Fig. 16-34. Letter file and easel.

Fig. 16-35. Letter file, working drawing.

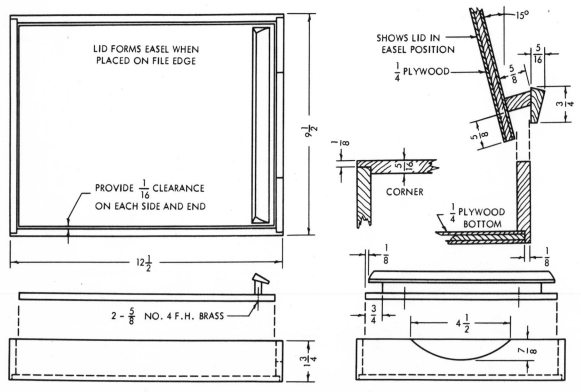

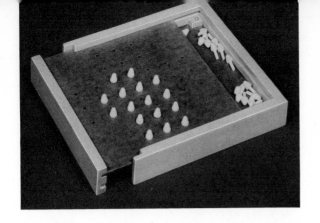

Fig. 16-37. Peg game box.

joints are cut. The rabbet for the bottom is not essential and the sides could be fitted around the bottom, using a butt joint.

PEG GAME BOX

This advanced project requires considerable skill to construct. Note how the top and one side can be pulled out to provide access to the pin storage. The adjustable friction screws hold the top in closed position.

Rip the strip of stock for the sides and plane it to exact size. Mount a single dado head blade on the table saw to cut the grooves. Use feather boards, Fig. 16-39, to insure accuracy and safety.

The rabbet joints can be cut following the procedure shown in Fig. 4-6, page 23. Prepare the hardboard panels and make a trial assembly. Glue the top to one side and the bottom to the other three sides. Make this glue-up in at least two stages — always reassembling the complete box after each application. Sand clearance in the "dry" grooves so the top will slide easily.

Install the auxiliary side, friction block and screw as final operations. A penetrating sealer is recommended for the finish.

Fig. 16-39. Cutting grooves in strip that will be used for sides. Note how feather boards are used to hold the strip snuggly against the table and fence.

Fig. 16-38. Peg game box, working drawing.

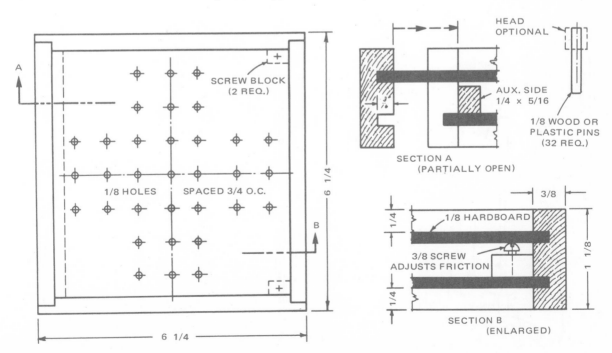

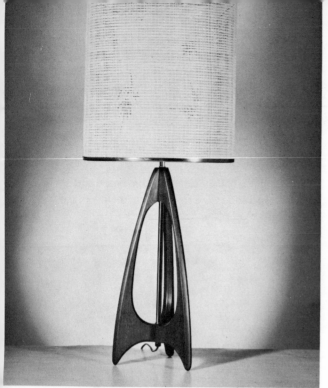

Fig. 16-40. Tripod lamp.

Fig. 16-42. Planing the joints with the leg clamped to a guide board.

TRIPOD LAMP

A beautiful lamp is shown in Fig. 16-40. The construction is not complicated, but it must be carefully done and finished, for when it is in use it will be well lighted and so near eye level that even slight flaws in workmanship will be quite noticeable. You should not attempt this project until you have had successful experience on several other wood projects.

Fig. 16-41. Tripod lamp, working drawing.

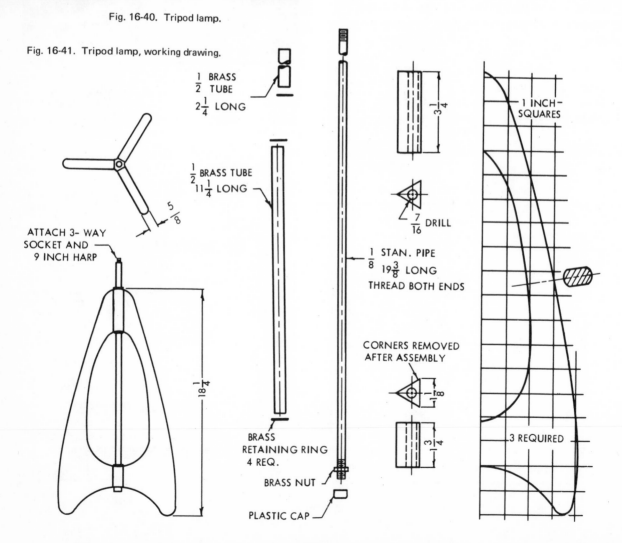

$\frac{1}{2}$ BRASS TUBE 2$\frac{1}{4}$ LONG

$\frac{1}{2}$ BRASS TUBE 11$\frac{1}{4}$ LONG

ATTACH 3- WAY SOCKET AND 9 INCH HARP

$\frac{5}{8}$

18$\frac{1}{4}$

$3\frac{1}{4}$

$\frac{7}{16}$ DRILL

$\frac{1}{8}$ STAN. PIPE 19$\frac{3}{8}$ LONG THREAD BOTH ENDS

CORNERS REMOVED AFTER ASSEMBLY

$\frac{1}{8}$

$3\frac{1}{4}$

1 INCH SQUARES

3 REQUIRED

BRASS RETAINING RING 4 REQ.

BRASS NUT

PLASTIC CAP

Select an attractive piece of wood and surface it carefully. Cut out the legs and plane the joining surfaces until they are flat and true, Fig. 16-42.

The triangular center pieces will be difficult to make by hand unless you build a jig to hold them while they are being planed, Fig. 11-3, page 59, shows a setup on the drill press that can be used to bore the holes.

Gluing the parts together will be easy if you cut out a jig like the one shown in Fig. 7-6, page 40. This holds the parts at the correct angle and also applies pressure. First, glue the triangular blocks to just one leg using the jig. After these joints have set, you can finish the gluing operation.

The shade shown in Fig. 16-40 is 14 in. in diameter and 15 in. high.

Fig. 16-43. Bookends.

BOOKENDS

Size: 3/4 x 5 x 7 3/8, Fig. 16-43.

Select an attractive kind of wood (walnut shown) and square it to size. Round the corners to a 1/2 in. radius and the edges to a 1/8 in. radius. Use sheet aluminum (1/16 x 4 1/2 x 5 1/2) for the base plate and attach it to the upright with three 3/4 in. FHB screws. Cutting a rabbet in the bottom of the upright will make a better fit.

Designs of your choice may be added. The bookends shown have overlays cut from sheet plastic. After applying finish, cover the base plates with "self-stik" flannel.

DESK PEN HOLDERS

Sizes: (left) 3/4 x 3 3/4 x 4 1/4
(center) 2 x 2 x 2
(right) 3/4 x 4 x 5 3/4, Fig. 16-44.

The holder shown on the left has a concave (dished-out) top surface about 1/4 in. deep. Form this surface with a gouge and then sand with coarse paper attached to the curved side of a rubber sanding block. See Fig. 5-9 and Fig. 9-4. Surfaces can be covered with 1/32 in. plastic laminate or left natural. Glue felt or cork disks to the bottom surface. Pen and holder units can be purchased at office supply stores and hobby shops.

Fig. 16-44. Desk pen holders.

NOTE CARD HOLDER

Fig. 16-45 shows a note card holder made from basswood and finished with a blond stain. It is designed to hold standard 4 x 6 in. cards. The length

Fig. 16-45. Note card holder.

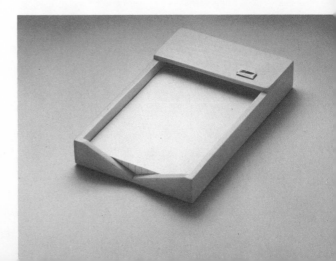

has been extended for better appearance and to provide space for optional mounting of pen or pencil holder.

Use 1/4 in. stock for sides and ends. Resaw thicker stock to secure this dimension as shown in Fig. 12-12, page 69. Square the bottom to size (allow 1/16 in. clearance for cards), then attach the sides and ends with glue. Use two pieces of tapered stock to form the open end.

CUTTING BOARD

Size: 1 x 5 1/4 x 7
      (feet) 1 in. diameter, Fig. 16-46.

Use a close grain hardwood for this project (birch and cherry are shown). It will be best to use a water-resistant glue to assemble the strips. See Fig. 7-1, page 38. The feet are turned from dowels as shown in Fig. 13-8, page 74. Finish with a penetrating sealer.

LETTER AND KEY RACK

Overall Size: 2 1/2 x 6 1/4 x 12, Fig. 16-47.
Compartment Fronts: 5/16 x 4 x 6 1/4.

Use 7/16 in. stock for the sides. The back and compartment fronts can be made of 5/16 in. solid stock or 1/4 in. plywood. Make a sub-assembly of the back and sides. Also make sub-assemblies of the compartment fronts. The compartment front consists of a strip glued to the inside bottom edge which forms the floor. Use screws to attach the compartment fronts to the sides.

Check the fit and then disassemble for final sanding and the application of finishes.

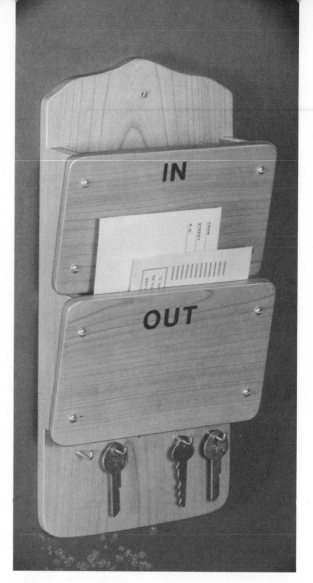

Fig. 16-47. Letter and key rack.

Fig. 16-46. Cutting board.

Fig. 16-48. Turned bowls and trays.

TURNED BOWLS AND TRAYS

Sizes: 2 1/2 to 7 in. diameters, Fig. 16-48.

These are all turned on a faceplate, following the procedure shown in Fig. 13-7, page 74. The thickness of stock varies from 1 to 2 in. If you plan to turn several of the same design, you should make a template to check your work.

Fig. 16-50. Twin server.

Form the holes in the top layer with internal cuts on the jig saw, Fig. 11-7, page 61. Sand the edges of the holes, glue base pieces together and square up edges. Cut out corners after edges are shaped. Turn the feet on the lathe as shown in Fig. 13-8, page 74.

WREN HOUSE

Use butt joints throughout and assemble wren house with weatherproof nails. When boring the entrance hole, be sure to clamp the stock across the grain to prevent splitting.

Stock for the front and back should be 1/2 in. thick. All other parts can be made from a 3/8 in. thickness. Redwood is recommended. Do not apply any type of finish.

Fig. 16-49. Salad fork and spoon.

SALAD FORK AND SPOON

Size: 2 1/2 x 10, Fig. 16-49.

The salad fork and spoon are cut from solid stock about 1 in. thick. Develop your design and then lay out the edge curve. Make the cuts on the band saw. Save the waste pieces and glue them back in place with just a few droplets of glue. Now lay out the top design and make the cuts on either the jig saw or band saw. Remove all the waste stock and form the finished shape with wood files and abrasive paper.

TWIN SERVER

Size: (base) 3/4 x 4 1/4 x 12
(feet) 3/4 in. diameter, Fig. 16-50.

Before making a working drawing of this project, secure the bowls so you will know how large to make the holes. The base is made of two layers of solid stock. The top layer is 5/16 in. thick and the bottom layer is 7/16 in. thick.

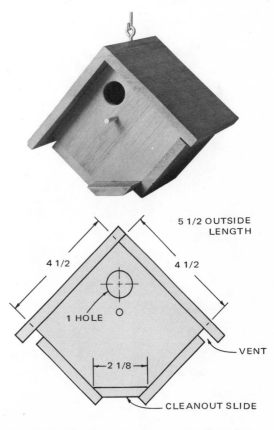

Fig. 16-51. Wren house. Drawing provides dimensions.

TILE TRIVET

Size: 6 1/2 x 6 1/2 x 1 1/4 high, Fig. 16-52.

A trivet is designed to protect table and cabinet tops from hot pans and dishes. First secure an attractive ceramic tile (6 x 6 in. size) and then build a frame in which it will fit. Use 1/4 in. plywood or hardboard for the bottom. Hold the tile in place when you glue-up the frame. The feet (as shown) are made from 3/4 in. wooden drawer pulls. You may want to turn them yourself, following the procedure shown in Fig. 13-8, page 74.

SOAP DISPENSER

Size: 2 3/4 x 4 1/2 x 12, Fig. 16-53.

This is a useful and decorative item for the bathroom. Because of the exposed edges it will be best to use 5/16 in. thick solid stock. The front panel cut out can be made on the jig saw as shown in Fig. 11-7, page 61. Edge and butt joints are used throughout.

To assemble, first make sub-assemblies of the front and sides; and the back and base. After the glue has set, these two units are fitted and assembled. Mount the dispenser firmly on the wall with two screws, one located at the top and one at the bottom.

Fig. 16-52. Above. Tile trivet. Fig. 16-53. Below. Soap dispenser.

Fig. 16-54. Desk organizer.

DESK ORGANIZER

Size: 5 1/4 x 11 wide x 11 1/2 high
(mail slots) 1 1/2 x 4 1/4, Fig. 16-54.

This cabinet of Early American design can be used on a desk or mounted on the wall. You should not attempt this project until you have had considerable experience. Although the parts are simple to cut out, the assembly requires careful work. You may want to eliminate the drawer.

Assemble the mail "pigeon holes" and two lower shelves as separate units. When complete, these units are joined to the sides. Attach the back next. The drawer is then constructed and fitted to the opening.

Fig. 16-55. Candy tray.

CANDY TRAY

Size: 3/4 x 6 1/4 x 12, Fig. 16-55.

After you have developed a pattern, lay it out on 5/8 in. stock and cut out the inside sections as shown in Fig. 11-8, page 61. Sand these edges and glue a 1/8 or 3/16 in. piece to the bottom. The outside contour is then cut and shaped. Be sure to sand the bottom and inside edges carefully before gluing, because inside corners are very difficult to work.

SOUVENIR PLATE HOLDER

Size: 5 x 7 1/2 sides, Fig. 16-56.

This project folds flat for storing or packaging. Use 1/4 in. or 5/16 in. solid stock. To save material, interlock the pattern layout as shown in Fig. 2-3, page 12. You may want to rough out each piece and fasten them together to make finish cuts, Fig. 11-7, page 61. Instead of hinges, try using small pieces of leather glued to the back edges.

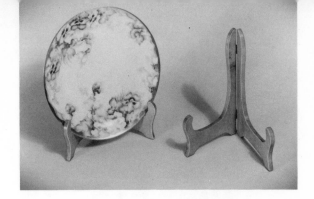

Fig. 16-56. Souvenir plate holder.

MUSICAL MANTELPIECE

Size: 3 1/4 x 5 3/4 x 10, Fig. 16-57.

The design resembles a church spire and forms an air chamber which amplifies the sound. The musical movement is mounted on the inside of the back — as high as practical. A miter joint (acute angle) should be used at the top. It can be cut on the band saw with the sides held on edge in a fixture attached to the miter gage. All material is 5/16 in. solid stock.

Fig. 16-57. Musical mantelpiece.

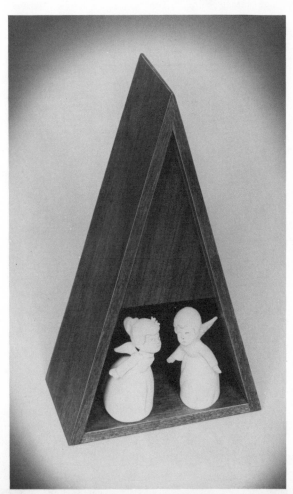

SCONCE

Size: (main body) 4 x 5 3/4 x 9 1/2
(handle) 1 1/8 x 3 3/4, Fig. 16-58.

Design is based on an Early American scoop — an important utensil in pioneer homes. Base is 3/8 in. stock, while sides and back are 5/16 in. thick. Candle holder and handle are turned as separate pieces on the lathe, Fig. 13-12, page 75. Attach these pieces to the base with a single screw set in the bottom of the candle hole and extending through the base and into the handle below. Edge and butt joints are assembled with glue and brads.

CARVED FIGURE

Size: 15 in. high, Fig. 16-59.

Develop an attractive design and select a soft-textured wood with an interesting grain pattern. Cut out the blank on the jig saw and then use spoke-shaves, chisels, files and sandpaper to complete the contours. Use metal pins made from nails to attach figure to base.

Fig. 16-60. Wall plaque.

Fig. 16-58. Sconce.

Fig. 16-59. Carved figure.

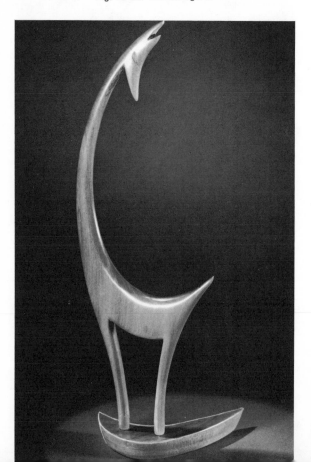

WALL PLAQUE

Size: 3/4 x 7 x 12, Fig. 16-60.

Develop your design and then make a full sized pattern. Use solid stock that has an attractive grain pattern (walnut shown). You may need to glue up several pieces to secure the desired width. Spend lots of time smoothing the edges after you cut out the design. Use a leather thong for hanging.

SPOOL HOLDER

Size: (base) 7/16 x 4 in. diameter, Fig. 16-61.
      (handle) 5/8 x 3 1/2 in. high
      (feet) 3/4 in. diameter

Make the base from 7/16 in. stock. After smoothing both surfaces with a plane, lay out the diameter and the 6 peg positions. See page 27. The feet can be turned on the lathe as shown in Fig. 13-8, page 74. The stem or handle is turned between centers. See page 73.

Fig. 16-61. Spool holder.

PULL TOY

Size: (body) 3/4 x 2 x 8, Fig. 16-62.
      (wheels) 1/2 x 1 3/4

Basswood was used to make the project shown. Use a jig saw or coping saw to cut out the body. Smooth and round the edges with coarse abrasive

Fig. 16-62. Pull toy.

paper or a wood file. The wheels can be turned by mounting a round blank on a lathe faceplate. See Fig. 13-11, page 75. The moving legs are somewhat difficult to lay out and assemble. Making a full-sized drawing of these parts will prove helpful. A shoelace makes a good pulling cord.

TIC-TAC-TOE GAME

Size: 13/16 x 3 3/8 x 5 3/8, Fig. 16-63.

Use 7/16 in. stock for the base and 3/8 in. stock for the game board overlay. Use saw kerfs to separate the game area. You can turn the pegs from an assembly made of 1/4 and 5/8 in. dowels. See Fig. 13-8, page 74. Peg storage holes in the ends of the base should provide a snug fit. Game area holes need to be slightly oversize so the pegs can be easily inserted and removed.

Fig. 16-63. Tic-tac-toe game.

SPINNING TOP

Size: (starting handle) 3/4 x 1 3/4 x 6 1/2
      (top) 3 1/2 in. diameter, Fig. 16-64.

This top will spin for two minutes or more. When making the starting handle, bore the holes before

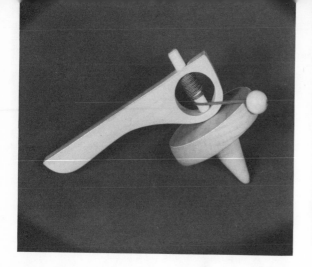

Fig. 16-64. Spinning top.

Fig. 16-65. Peg game.

cutting out the shape. The conical turning of the top can be eliminated and the 3/8 in. dowel extended down to form the spinning point. Make the starter cord from a shoe string and wooden bead. Wax the bearings for best performance.

PEG GAME

Size: 1 x 5 x 5, Fig. 16-65.

Base is formed by framing 1/2 or 3/4 in. particle board with 5/16 in. solid stock. Use rabbet or miter joints at the corners. Cover the top surface of the

particle board with 1/32 in. plastic laminate. The plastic pegs shown were purchased at a school supply store.

SERVING TRAY

Size: 2 x 11 x 17, Fig. 16-66.

Use an attractive piece of 1/4 in. plywood and matching solid stock. Sides are 5/16 in. thick and ends are 1/2 in. thick. Cut grooves in sides and ends as shown in Fig. 12-15, page 69. Since it is easier to cut a groove all the way through, follow the suggestion shown in the drawing.

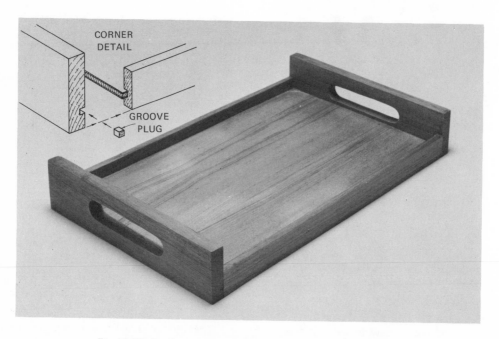

Fig. 16-66. Serving tray. Inset drawing shows construction detail.

GLOSSARY

Here are some words that apply to woodworking and wood finishing, in addition to the ones used and defined in the instructional units.

ADHESIVE: A substance used to hold materials together by surface attachment. It is a general term that includes cements, glue, paste or mucilage.

ALIGN: To bring parts into proper position with each other.

ALUMINUM OXIDE: (Al_2O_3), an abrasive made by fusing Bauxite clay in an electric furnace. Used in the manufacture of grinding wheels, sharpening stones, and abrasive papers.

ARBOR: A short shaft or spindle on which another rotating part is mounted.

ARRIS: An outside corner or edge formed by the meeting of two surfaces.

BLEACHING: Lightening the color of wood by applying a chemical solution.

BLEEDING: The movement of stain or dye from the wood into surface coats. For example, a white enamel applied over a mahogany oil stain will bleed (develop pink spots).

BLUE STAIN: A stain caused by a fungus growth in unseasoned lumber. Often found in pine. It does not affect the strength of the wood.

BURL: A swirl or twist in the grain of the wood, usually near a knot.

CALIPER: A tool for measuring the diameter of circular work.

CHECKS: Small splits running parallel to the wood grain, usually caused by improper seasoning.

CHUCK: A broad term meaning a device for holding a rotating tool or work during an operation.

CLEAT: A strip of wood fastened to another piece, usually to provide a holding or bracing effect.

CLINCH: Nails made to hold more securely by bending down the ends of the protruding nails.

COUNTERBORING: To enlarge a hole through part of its length by boring.

COUNTERSINKING: To recess a hole conically for the head of a screw or bolt.

CORE: The center of a plywood panel. Plywood cores may be of either sawn lumber or veneer.

DADO: A groove cut across the grain of a board.

DUTCHMAN: A piece fitted into the work to cover a defect or error.

EARTH PIGMENTS: Pigments mined from the earth such as ochre, umber, sienna and vandyke brown.

FACE PLATE: A circular plate that can be attached to the headstock spindle of the lathe.

FENCE: An adjustable metal bar or strip mounted on the table of a machine or tool to guide the work.

FIGURE: The pattern produced in a wood surface by the annual growth rings, wood rays and knots.

FLOCK: Shredded cloth fibers. They are applied to a surface with a special adhesive to form a soft, felt-like finish.

GLUE BLOCKS: Small blocks of wood, usually triangular in shape, that are glued along the inside corner of a joint to add strength.

HARDBOARD: A material made by exploding (a steam process) wood chips into wood fibers and forming them into sheets, using heat and pressure.

HOLIDAYS: Areas of surface missed by a painter.

INLAY: A decoration where the design is set into the wood surface.

JIG: A device which holds the work and/or guides the tool while forming or assembling wood parts.

KERF: The slit or space made by the blade of any hand or power saw.

KNOT: Cross section of a branch or limb imbedded in the wood during the growth of the tree.

LAC: A natural resin secreted by insects that live on the sap of certain trees in oriental countries. The base for shellac.

LAMINATE: To build up wood in layers. Each layer is called a lamination or ply. The grain may run in the same direction in each lamination or may be turned at a right angle.

LINEAR: Pertaining to a line or consisting of lines. Linear measure refers to measurement along the length.

LINSEED OIL: A vegetable oil pressed from the seeds of the flax plant. Used extensively in the manufacture of oil base paints and finishes.

MANDREL: A shaft or spindle on which an object may be mounted for rotation.

MARQUETRY: An ornamental surface built up of various wood veneers to form a pattern or picture. Usually cut on the jig saw.

MESH: Openings formed by crossing or weaving threads, strings or wire.

MINERAL SPIRITS: A petroleum solvent used as a

substitute for turpentine.

MITER or MITRE: The joining of two pieces at an evenly divided angle. A cut made at an angle, usually 45 degrees.

OXIDIZE: To unite with oxygen — a chemical reaction.

PIGMENT: Finely ground powders that are insoluble and provide color and body to a finishing material.

PLAIN-SAWED: Lumber that is cut on a tangent to the annular growth rings.

QUARTER-SAWED: Lumber that is cut at approximately a 90 degree angle to the annular growth rings.

QUILL: The movable sleeve that carries the bearings and spindle of the drill press.

RABBET: A cut made in the edge of a board to form a joint with another piece.

RATCHET: A gear with triangular-shaped teeth that are engaged by a pawl, which imparts intermittent motion or locks it against backward movement.

RELATIVE HUMIDITY: The ratio of water vapor actually present in the air as related to the greatest amount of vapor the air can carry at a given temperature.

ROTARY CUT: A method of cutting veneer where the entire log is centered in a huge lathe and turned against a broad knife.

RPM: An abbreviation for revolutions per minute.

RUNS: Also called "sags" and "curtains." Irregularities in a surface finish usually caused by too heavy an application.

SABER SAWING: Cutting with a special blade mounted in only the lower chuck of the jig saw. Also applies to cutting with a portable saber saw.

SHAKE: A defect in wood running parallel to the grain caused by the separation of the spring and summer growth rings.

SILICON CARBIDE (Si C): Produced by fusing silica (sand) and coke at high temperatures. Used as an abrasive and sold under such trade names as Carborundum and Crystolon.

SLICED: A method of cutting veneer where a section of a log is thrust down along a knife edge that sheers off the veneer in sheets.

SPLAYED: Forming an oblique angle in the joining of two parts. Applies to the leg of a table or chair that make an angle in two directions with the top or seat.

SPLINE: A thin strip of wood inserted in matching grooves cut on the joining faces of a joint. Also, a flexible rod or rule used to draw curved lines.

STEAMED: This term, when applied to walnut lumber, refers to a process where the green lumber is steamed in vats for the purpose of darkening the sapwood.

STRAIGHTEDGE: A straight strip of wood or metal with opposite faces parallel. Used to lay out and check the accuracy of work.

TAPER: A gradual and uniform decrease in the size of a hole, cylinder, or rectangular part.

TEMPLATE: A pattern, guide or model that is used to lay out work or check its accuracy.

THINNERS: Volatile liquids that are used to regulate the consistency (thickness) of finishing materials.

TONGUE: A projecting bead cut on the edge of a board that fits into a groove on another piece.

TRACKING: Refers to the alignment of a blade as it runs on the band saw wheel.

TURPENTINE: A volatile solvent used in wood finishes, which is made by distilling the gum obtained from the pine tree.

VEHICLE: The liquid part of a paint.

VENEER: A thin sheet of wood, either sliced, cut or sawn. Veneer may be referred to as a ply when assembled in a panel.

VOLATILE: A liquid that dries rapidly by evaporation.

WANE: The presence of bark, or the lack of wood from any cause on the edge or corner of a piece of lumber.

WARP: Any variation from a true or plane surface. It may include bow, cup, crook or wind (twist).

WATER STAIN: Colored dyes that are soluble in water.

WATER WHITE: Transparent like water. Used to describe a very clear lacquer or varnish.

ACKNOWLEDGMENTS

The author wishes to express his sincere appreciation to the following companies and organizations for the valuable information and photographs that they provided:

Adjustable Clamp Co., Chicago, IL
American Forest Products Industries, Washington, DC
American Plywood Assoc., Tacoma, WA
Binks Manufacturing Co., Chicago, IL
Black & Decker Mfg. Co., Towson, MD
Bostitch, Div. of Textron, East Greenwich, RI
Caradco Corp., Rantoul, IL
DeVilbiss Co., Toledo, OH
Ekstrom, Carlson and Co., Rockford, IL
Forest Products Laboratory, Madison, WI
Georgia-Pacific Corp., Portland, OR
Greenlee Tool Co., Rockford, IL
International Paper Co., Longview, WA
Iowa Paint Manufacturing Co., Des Moines, IA

Jenkins, Div. of Kohler-General, Sheboygan Falls, WI
Jensen Incorporated, Farmington, MI
Masonite Corp., Chicago, IL
Mattison Machine Works, Rockford, IL
Merillat Industries, Inc., Adrian, MI
Mersman Brothers Corp., Celina, OH
Millers Falls Co., Greenfield, MA
National Forest Products Assoc., Washington, DC
Norton Co., Worcester, MA
Paxton Lumber Co., Des Moines, IA
H. K. Porter Co., Inc., Pittsburgh, PA
Rockwell International, Pittsburgh, PA
Sherwin-Williams Co., Cleveland, OH
Stanley Tools, The Stanley Works, New Britain, CT
Thomasville Furniture Industries, Thomasville, NC
Viking Pump Co., Cedar Falls, IA
Western Wood Products Assoc., Portland, OR
Westvaco, New York, NY
Weyerhaeuser Co., Tacoma, WA

FOR YOUR FURTHER STUDY

Capron, J. H., WOOD LAMINATING, McKnight Publishing Co., Bloomington, Illinois.

Cramlet, Ross C., WOODWORK VISUALIZED, Glencoe Publishing Co., Encino, California.

Cunningham, Beryl M., and Holthrop, Wm. F., WOODSHOP TOOL MAINTENANCE , Chas. A. Bennett Co., Peoria, Illinois.

Feirer, John L., and Hutchings, Gilbert, ADVANCED WOODWORK AND FURNITURE MAKING, Chas. A. Bennett Co., Peoria, Illinois.

Feirer, John L., WOODWORKING FOR INDUSTRY, Chas, A. Bennett Co., Peoria, Illinois.

Groneman, Chris H., GENERAL WOODWORKING, McGraw-Hill Co., New York, New York.

Groneman, Chris H. and Glazener, Everett R., TECHNICAL WOODWORKING, Webster Division, McGraw-Hill Co., New York, New York.

Hammond, James J. and others, WOODWORKING TECHNOLOGY, McKnight Publishing Co., Bloomington, Illinois.

Hunt, De Witt, SHOP TOOLS, CARE AND REPAIR, D. Van Nostrand Co., Princeton, New Jersey.

Klenke, William W., THE ART OF WOOD TURNING, Chas. A. Bennett Co., Peoria, Illinois.

Lindbeck, John R., DESIGN TEXTBOOK, McKnight Publishing Co., Bloomington, Illinois.

McGinnis, Harry and Ruley, M. J., BASIC WOODWORK PROJECTS, McKnight Publishing Co., Bloomington, Illinois.

Olson, Delmar W., WOODS AND WOODWORKING, Prentice-Hall, Inc., Englewood Cliffs, New Jersey.

Smith, Robert E., MACHINE WOODWORKING, McKnight Publishing Co., Bloomington, Illinois.

Soderberg, George A., FINISHING TECHNOLOGY, McKnight Publishing Co., Bloomington, Illinois.

Wagner, Willis H., MODERN CARPENTRY, The Goodheart-Willcox Co., South Holland, Illinois.

Wagner, Willis H., MODERN WOODWORKING, Goodheart-Willcox Co., South Holland, Illinois.

Zimmerman, Fred W., EXPLORING WOODWORKING, The Goodheart-Willcox Co., South Holland, Illinois.

Useful Information

CONVERSION TABLE
METRIC TO ENGLISH

WHEN YOU KNOW	MULTIPLY BY: * = Exact		TO FIND
	VERY ACCURATE	APPROXIMATE	
LENGTH			
millimetres	0.0393701	0.04	inches
centimetres	0.3937008	0.4	inches
metres	3.280840	3.3	feet
metres	1.093613	1.1	yards
kilometres	0.621371	0.6	miles
WEIGHT			
grains	0.00228571	0.0023	ounces
grams	0.03527396	0.035	ounces
kilograms	2.204623	2.2	pounds
tonnes	1.1023113	1.1	short tons
VOLUME			
millilitres		0.2	teaspoons
millilitres	0.06667	0.067	tablespoons
millilitres	0.03381402	0.03	fluid ounces
litres	61.02374	61.024	cubic inches
litres	2.113376	2.1	pints
litres	1.056688	1.06	quarts
litres	0.26417205	0.26	gallons
litres	0.03531467	0.35	cubic feet
cubic metres	61023.74	61023.7	cubic inches
cubic metres	35.31467	35.0	cubic feet
cubic metres	1.3079506	1.3	cubic yards
cubic metres	264.17205	264.0	gallons
AREA			
square centimetres	0.1550003	0.16	square inches
square centimetres	0.00107639	0.001	square feet
square metres	10.76391	10.8	square feet
square metres	1.195990	1.2	square yards
square kilometres		0.4	square miles
hectares	2.471054	2.5	acres
TEMPERATURE			
Celsius	*9/5 (then add 32)		Fahrenheit

Useful Information

CONVERSION TABLE
ENGLISH TO METRIC

WHEN YOU KNOW ⬇	MULTIPLY BY: * = Exact		TO FIND ⬇
	VERY ACCURATE	APPROXIMATE	
LENGTH			
inches	* 25.4		millimetres
inches	* 2.54		centimetres
feet	* 0.3048		metres
feet	* 30.48		centimetres
yards	* 0.9144	0.9	metres
miles	* 1.609344	1.6	kilometres
WEIGHT			
grains	15.43236	15.4	grams
ounces	* 28.349523125	28.0	grams
ounces	* 0.028349523125	.028	kilograms
pounds	* 0.45359237	0.45	kilograms
short ton	* 0.90718474	0.9	tonnes
VOLUME			
teaspoons		5.0	millilitres
tablespoons		15.0	millilitres
fluid ounces	29.57353	30.0	millilitres
cups		0.24	litres
pints	* 0.473176473	0.47	litres
quarts	* 0.946352946	0.95	litres
gallons	* 3.785411784	3.8	litres
cubic inches	* 0.016387064	0.02	litres
cubic feet	* 0.028316846592	0.03	cubic metres
cubic yards	* 0.764554857984	0.76	cubic metres
AREA			
square inches	* 6.4516	6.5	square centimetres
square feet	* 0.09290304	0.09	square metres
square yards	* 0.83612736	0.8	square metres
square miles		2.6	square kilometres
acres	* 0.40468564224	0.4	hectares
TEMPERATURE			
Fahrenheit	* 5/9 (after subtracting 32)		Celsius

INDEX

A

Abrasive paper, 45, 46
  kinds and grades, 45, 46
  using, 46, 47
Acknowledgments, 115
Arcs and circles, 27
Auger bit, sharpening, 32, 33
Auger bits and braces, 32
Awl, scratch, 33

B

Backsaw, 19
Band saw, 58, 61
  cutting on, 62
  safety rules, 62, 63
Bar clamps, 39
Bevels, forming, 27, 30, 31
Bill of materials, 8
Bit,
  auger, 32
  expansive, 35
  Forstner, 35
Block plane, 19
Board footage, 11, 12
Bookends, 105
Bookrack, 91, 92
Boring holes, 32, 33
  at angle, 34, 35
Bowls and trays, turned, 107
Box, trinket, 89, 90
Brace and auger bit, 32
Bridge set, 96
Brushes, 51
Butt joints, 21, 22

C

Calendar, desk, 105
Candelabra, 98
Candy tray, 109
Card box, 6, 78
Careers,
  construction, 87
  distribution, 87
  forestry, 85
  lumbering, 85

manufacturing, 85, 87
  opportunities, 85
  wood science and
    technology, 88
Carved figure, 110
Carving, 30
Chamfers, forming, 27, 30, 31
Chisel, 24, 25
  safety rule, 31
Chisels, wood turning, 72
Circles and arcs, 27
Circular saw, 64, 66
  cutting rabbets, 69
  cutting to length, 68
  dado head, 69
  resawing, 68
  ripping, 66, 67
  safety rules, 69, 70
Clamping wood, 37
Clamps, bar, 39
Clamps, wood, 40
Coaster set, 97
Construction,
  career opportunities, 87
Conversion tables, 116, 117
Coping saw, 29
Counterboring, 34
Countersinking screw, 43
Cracker tray, 94
Curves,
  cutting, 28, 29
  forming, 27
  sanding, 47
  smoothing, 29
Cutting
  board, 106
  curves, 28, 29
  on band saw, 62
  on jig saw, 59, 60
  rabbets with the grain, 69
Cutting stock to
  length, 68
  rough length, 13

D

Dado head, 69
Dado joints, 21, 24, 25
Dados and grooves, 24, 25
Design, project, 5
Desk organizer, 109
Desk pen holders, 105
Distribution,
  career opportunities, 87
Dividers, 27
Dovetail saw, 20
Dowel joints, 21, 23
Doweling jig, 22, 23
Drawings, working, 6, 7
Drill press, 58
Drilling holes, 32, 35
  for wood screws, 43

E

Early American tray, 101
Edge joints, 21, 22
Edge, planing, 18
Enamel, 55
End grain, planing, 19
English to metric conversion
  table, 117
Expansive bit, 35

F

Faceplate, mounting work, 73
Faceplate turning, 74
Fasteners, metal, 41
Fasteners, special, 44
Feather board, 66, 69
Figure, carved, 110
Finished dimensions,
  planing and sawing, 15
Finished surfaces,
  sanding and rubbing, 55, 56
Finishes, safety rules, 52
Finishing in industry, 57
Finishing schedules, 56, 57
Finishing, wood, 50
Forest products, 77
Forestry, career opportunities, 85

Fork and spoon, salad, 107
Forstner bit, 35

G

Game, peg, 103, 112
Game, tic-tac-toe, 111
General safety rules, 9, 13, 31, 52
  60, 62, 63, 65, 69, 70, 76
Glossary, 113, 114
Glue,
  mixing powdered, 38
  polyvinyl resin emulsion, 37
  resorcinol resin, 37
  setting time, 39
  spread, 38
  urea-formaldehyde resin, 37
Gluing wood, 37
Gouge, 30
Grinding a plane iron, 16
Groove joints, 21, 24, 25

H

Hammers, 41
Hand drill, 36
Hardboard, 80
Hardwood lumber, 10
Holes, drilling and boring, 32
Honing plane iron, 15, 16

I

Industry, finishing, 57
Installing blade in jig saw, 60, 61

J

Jack plane, 18
Jig saw, 58, 59
  cutting on, 59, 60
  installing blade, 60, 61
Jointer, 64
  adjusting, 64, 65
  safety rules, 65
  size limitations, 66
Jointing an edge, 65
Joints, cleaning, 38, 39
Joints, wood, 21

K

Key and letter rack, 106

L

Lacquer, 54
Lamp, cube, 92, 93
Lamp, tripod, 104
Lap joints, 21, 25, 26
Lathe,
  chisels, 72
  safety rules, 76
  special chucking
    and mounting, 74, 75

tool rest, 72
  wood, 71
Laying out, 12
Letter and key rack, 106
Letter file and easel, 102
Lumber, 77
  uses, 83, 84
Lumbering, 78, 79
  as a career, 85

M

Mantelpiece, musical, 109
Manufacturing, career
  opportunity, 85, 87
Marking gage, 25
Materials, bill of, 8
Metal fasteners, 41
Metric conversions, 116, 117
Metric to English
  conversion table, 117
Miter box, 26
Miter joints, 21, 26
Moisture content, 77, 78
Mortise and tenon joints, 21, 26
Musical mantelpiece, 109

N

Nails, 41, 42
Napkin holder, 95
Note card holder, 105

O

Occupational opportunities, 85
Organizer, desk, 109

P

Paint, 55
Particleboard, 80, 82
Paste filler, 52, 53
Patterns, 27, 28
Peg game, 103, 112
Penetrating sealer, 54, 55
Pen holders, desk, 105
Pictorial sketch, 5, 6
Plan of procedure, 7
Plane,
  adjusting, 16, 17
  block, 19
  iron, grinding, 16
  iron, honing, 15, 16
  jack, 18
  parts, 15
  rabbet, 24
  router, 25
Planing a surface, 17, 65, 66
Planing an edge, 18
Planing end grain, 19

Planing stock to
  finished dimensions, 15
Planning work, 4
Plaque, wall, 111
Plastic wood, 48
Plate holder, 109
Plywood, 11, 80, 81
Polyvinyl resin emulsion glue, 37
Preparing for finish, 45
Procedure, plan of, 7
Project design, 5
Projects, 89
  selecting, 4
Pull toy, 111
Push drill, 36
Push sticks, 63, 66, 67

R

Rabbet joints, 21, 23, 24
Rabbet plane, 24
Repairing wood surface, 48, 49
Resawing, 68
Resorcinol resin glue, 37
Ripping stock to
  rough width, 13
  width, 66, 67
Roughing-out stock, 10
Router plane, 25
Rubbing finished surfaces, 55, 56
Rules, safety, 9, 13, 31, 52, 60,
  62, 63, 65, 69, 70, 76

S

Safety rules, 9, 13, 31, 52, 60,
  62, 63, 65, 69, 70, 76
  band saw, 62, 63
  chisel, 31
  circular saw, 69, 70
  finishes, 52
  jointer, 65
  lathe, 76
  sawing, 13
Salad fork and spoon, 107
Sanding, 45
  board, 20, 47
  curve, 47
  finished surfaces, 55, 56
  lathe work, 74
  small pieces, 47
Saw,
  back, 19
  band, 58, 61
  circular, 64, 66
  coping, 29
  crosscut, 13

dovetail, 20
jig, 58, 59
rip, 13
teeth, 12
Sawing, safety rule, 13
Sawing stock to
 finished dimensions, 15
Schedules, finishing, 56, 57
Sconce, 110
Scratch awl, 33
Screwdrivers, 43, 44
Screws, drilling holes for, 43
Screws, wood, 42, 43
Sealer, penetrating, 54, 55
Sealers, 53
Selecting projects, 4
Selecting stock, 10, 12
Server, twin, 107
Shaping, 30
Sharpening auger bit, 32, 33
Size, lumber, 11
Sketch, pictorial, 5, 6
Smoothing curves, 29
Snack tray, 112
Soap dispenser, 108
Softwood lumber, 10
Souvenir plate holder, 109
Spindle turning, 71, 72, 73
 mounting stock, 71, 72

Spinning top, 111
Spokeshave, 29
Spool holder, 111
Spoon and fork, salad, 107
Spoon rack, 99
Squaring end of stock, 18
Squaring small parts, 19, 20
Staining, 51
Stock, selecting, 10, 12
Stock, roughing-out, 10
Stool, 100
Surface, lumber, 11
Surface, planing, 17
Synthetic varnish, 54

T

Tapers, 31
Templates, 27, 28
Tic-tac-toe game, 111
Tile trivet, 108
Top, spinning, 111
Trammel points, 27
Tray,
 candy, 109
 cracker, 94
 Early American, 101
 serving, 112
Trays and bowls, turned, 107
Trinket box, 89, 90
Tripod lamp, 104

Trivet, tile, 108
Turned bowls and trays, 107
Twin server, 107

U

Urea-formaldehyde resin glue, 37

V

Varnish, synthetic, 54
Veneer, 80

W

Wall plaque, 111
Wood, 77
 clamps, 40
 finishing, 50
 glues, 37
 growth, 77
 joints, 21
 kinds of, 10
 lathe, 71
 moisture content, 77, 78
 science and technology, 88
 scraper, 47
 screws, 42, 43
 shrinkage, 77, 78
 structure, 77
Woodworking machines,
 safety rules, 60
Work, planning, 4
Working drawings, 6, 7
Wren house, 107